Editor

Diana Herweck, Psy.D.

Editorial Project Manager

Dona Herweck Rice

Editor-in-Chief

Sharon Coan, M.S. Ed.

Illustrator

Kevin Barnes

Cover Artist

Barb Lorseyedi

Art Coordinator

Kevin Barnes

Imaging

Alfred Lau

Rosa C. See

Product Manager

Phil Garcia

Publishers

Rachelle Cracchiolo, M.S. Ed.

Mary Dupuy Smith, M.S. Ed.

Comprehension & Critical Thinking

LEVEL 5

Includes Document-Based Questions

Author

Sarah Kartchner Clark

Reading passages provided by *TIME For Kids* magazine.

Teacher Created Materials, Inc.

6421 Industry Way

Westminster, CA 92683

www.teachercreated.com

ISBN-0-7439-3375-3

©2002 Teacher Created Materials, Inc.

Made in U.S.A.

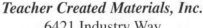

Teacher Created Materials

Table of Contents

Introduction

We live in a day of increased accountability and standards-based instruction. Teachers are feeling the pressure to have their students perform well on standardized tests. As educators, we know that students need more than just practice on answering questions and how to take tests. Students need thinking skills to back up what they are being taught in school. Every teacher knows that students who can comprehend what they read, and then apply information they learn to real-life situations not only score better on tests, but perform better in life.

So how can we help our students find success in taking standardized tests as well as being problem solvers for life? One way is to build students' reading comprehension and critical thinking skills. This unit has been specifically designed to build such skills. It has been written with the student in mind. This unit will provide your students with the experience of reading, comprehending, analyzing, and problem solving issues that are taking place in their world today.

The *Comprehension and Critical Thinking* series is a tool that will help teachers teach comprehension and critical thinking skills to their students and enable their students to perform better in both a test and real-world setting. This series provides motivating, readable, interesting, nonfiction text, as well as exercises to help students practice comprehension and critical thinking skills while becoming better readers.

The General Lesson Plan

Each lesson plan begins with a nonfiction article that has been written specifically for your students. These articles are written at the readability level of your students so that the vocabulary doesn't interfere with the comprehension of what is being read. These high-interest nonfiction articles are from *TIME For Kids* authors. Here is a suggestion of the general lesson plan:

Step 1—Students read a nonfiction article from *TIME For Kids* authors.

Step 2—Students answer questions about the article they have just read. These questions are written using Bloom's Taxonomy as a guide. Questions begin with basic comprehension and increase in complexity and higher level thinking.

Step 3—Students study a primary source document (such as maps, census reports, graphs, cartoons, charts, and diagrams) that is related to the article.

Step 4—Students demonstrate critical thinking skills by responding to document-based questions.

Step 5—Students continue demonstrating critical thinking skills by participating in activities based on the documents.

Introduction (cont.)

What Is Bloom's Taxonomy?

The questions that follow each passage in *Comprehension and Critical Thinking* assess all levels of learning by following Bloom's Taxonomy, a six-level classification system for comprehension questions devised by Benjamin Bloom in 1956. The questions are always presented in order, progressing from knowledge to evaluation.

The skills listed for each level are essential to keep in mind when teaching comprehension to assure that your students reach the higher levels of thinking. Use this classification to form your own questions whenever your students listen to or read material.

Level 1: Knowledge—At this level, students are asked to recall information or find requested information in an article. They will demonstrate remembering, recognizing, and describing. Question cues associated with the knowledge level include *who, what, when, where, why, how, collect, examine, quote, name, identify, show, define, tell,* and *list.*

Level 2: Comprehension—At this level, students begin to interpret what is being read. This means they can find information that is stated in a different way than the question. They will demonstrate translating, putting into one's own words, organizing and selecting facts. Question cues associated with the comprehension level include *summarize, associate, estimate, extend, discuss, interpret, contrast, predict, give examples, explain,* and *describe.*

Level 3: Application—At this level, students use the information that has been read. They apply the knowledge to new settings and situations. Students solve problems using their knowledge and skills. Question cues associated with the application level include *apply, experiment, modify, relate, illustrate, demonstrate, solve, construct, change, discover, complete,* and *calculate.*

Level 4: Analysis—At this level, students begin to see patterns and the organization of parts. Students are able to recognize hidden meanings. Question cues associated with the analysis level include *analyze, organize, order, divide, compare, select, infer, classify, arrange, connect, separate,* and *cause and effect.*

Level 5: Synthesis—At this level, students begin to compare and discriminate between ideas presented. They pull knowledge together to create new ideas. Students are able to generalize from a set of facts, and they can relate their new knowledge to other areas. Question cues associated with the synthesis level include *predict, draw conclusions, integrate, combine, invent, prepare, rewrite, generalize, plan, create, what if...* and *design.*

Level 6: Evaluation—At the highest level of Bloom's Taxonomy, students can make a judgement based on a predetermined set of criteria. They can assess the value of theories and can form opinions and defend them. Students can verify the value of evidence presented. Question cues associated with the evaluation level include *test, rank, grade, decide, assess, recommend, convince, select, measure, discriminate, support, conclude, compare, summarize, judge,* and *determine.*

Introduction *(cont.)*

What Are Primary Source Documents?

Primary source documents are graphics or materials that we find in our everyday lives. These documents provide information that can aid in solving problems and extend comprehension. You will find samples of primary source documents following each *TIME For Kids* article. These documents are related to the topics addressed in the articles. They provide students with another way to look at information and knowledge on a given topic. Here is a list of primary source documents that may be used in the *Comprehension and Critical Thinking* series:

charts	obituaries
graphs	poetry
diagrams	wills
geographical maps	money
political maps	tax records
town/city maps	historical documents
state/country maps	pictures of people
diaries	pictures of clothing
letters	pictures of landscapes
newspaper articles	signs
political cartoons	games
speeches	census records
treaties	advertisements
flags	encyclopedia articles
recipes	magazine articles

Primary source documents can be useful at all grade levels. They enable you to share information in a variety of formats. Students are bombarded with facts and information from varied sources, ranging from their textbooks to the news they watch on television. Understanding how to sift through and analyze this information will increase your students' critical thinking as well as survival skills.

How Can I Use Primary Source Documents?

Use the questions that follow each primary source document in this series. Allow time for students to observe and analyze the documents without answering the questions. The questions will focus them in a specific direction. Encourage students to make observations of their own. After this, move on to the document-based questions that follow the documents. Be sure to allow time for class or small-group discussion. This will give students the opportunity to think aloud, as well as hear other viewpoints or ideas.

Look for opportunities to incorporate other primary source documents with subjects you are studying in class. You will find your students recognizing and analyzing these sources of information in their daily lives. Using primary source documents can provide your students with opportunities to read and understand information presented in different ways. Primary source documents will help your students learn to live in the world around them.

Introduction *(cont.)*

What Are Document-Based Questions?

Document-based questions (DBQ) are a major focus in schools today. Once found only on advanced placement tests for high school students, document-based questions are finding themselves on standardized tests for elementary school students. The goal of document-based questions is to raise standards of teaching and learning in all schools.

Students are tested on their ability to analyze a set of documents, use their prior knowledge, and come up with answers to the document-based questions. This higher level questioning is meant to get at higher level thinking skills.

For the *Comprehension and Critical Thinking* series, students are asked to look over a document and answer a series of questions about it. Known as "scaffolding" questions, they are designed to help the student build a foundation of understanding which can be used to write an essay or answer more analytical questions.

How Can I Introduce My Students to Document-Based Questions?

There are many things you can do to introduce your students to primary source documents and document-based questions. Here are some suggestions:

- Begin a collection of documents that can be used for document-based questions. You can find samples of documents to use practically everywhere. Collect maps, diagrams, charts, historical documents, letters, cards, announcements, signs, etc. Encourage your students to be on the lookout for them as well. Post these in your classroom, or designate a special spot for your collection. Spend a few minutes each day analyzing them and discussing them as a class or in small groups.

- After reading a newspaper or magazine article with your students, share observations. Encourage your students to analyze what the article said. What was the message of the author?

- Quiz students on what they read in their textbooks, but don't just ask them to recall questions. Ask questions that require them to use some critical thinking skills.

- After watching a movie, compare and contrast characters with your students. Analyze events in the movie. How do the characters change over a certain period of time?

- Make primary source documents of your own. Make a time line of events your students have done this year in school. Take a survey of favorite subjects in school, and then graph the results. Create a map of the school and design the best possible fire escape routes. Have students be ready to explain their findings and their reasoning.

Introduction (cont.)

How Can You Build Comprehension?

Once you have an understanding of document-based questions and Bloom's Taxonomy, you are ready to implement skills that will increase the comprehension of your students. Increasing comprehension is the goal of every teacher, but there are many obstacles. Identifying and understanding these obstacles can eliminate the problems. Here is a list of common comprehension problems:

- For some students, comprehension can be inhibited because the reading level of the material is too high. Before assigning a reading assignment for students, check to be sure that the readability of the material is appropriate for your students.

- There might be vocabulary words that are hard to decipher. Sometimes one word can eliminate comprehension of an entire paragraph. Teach your students how to use context clues to determine the meaning of words.

- You may have limited English speakers in your classroom, or students with disabilities that would prevent them from comprehending what is being read. Make adjustments as needed to accommodate these needs.

- Lack of interest or motivation for what is being read can lead to low comprehension as well. Take a minute to jot down the interests of each individual student. Can you locate reading materials that your students would find interesting? This will aid comprehension as well as motivation.

There are many skills needed to form the complex activity of comprehension. This wide range of understanding and ability develops over time in competent readers. The following list includes traditional skills found in scope-and-sequence charts and standards for reading comprehension.

identifies details	classifies places into categories
recognizes the main idea	compares and contrasts
recognizes hidden meaning	draws conclusions
determines sequence	makes generalizations
recalls details	recognizes paragraph organization
locates reference	predicts outcome
recalls the gist of story	recognizes hyperbole and exaggeration
labels parts	experiences empathy for a character
summarizes	experiences an emotional reaction to text
recognizes anaphoric relationships	judges quality/appeal of text
identifies time sequence	judges author's qualifications
describes a character	recognizes facts vs. opinions
retells story in own words	applies understanding to new situations
infers main idea	recognizes figurative language
infers details	identifies mood
infers cause and effect	identifies plot and story line
infers author's purpose/intent	identifies characters

Introduction *(cont.)*

How Can You Build Critical Thinking Skills?

Teaching students to think critically can be challenging and exciting. Students usually think in a certain way. In some ways we have trained students to think of right or wrong answers instead of thinking there might be more than one answer to solve a problem. We need to provide students with opportunities to "think outside the box." The best resource for teaching your students to use critical thinking is YOU!

What types of questions do you ask your students? Are you always asking them basic knowledge and comprehension questions, looking only for recall of information? How much of your school day do you spend encouraging your students to solve problems for themselves and to look at alternative answers?

Thinking critically requires students to use new information, prior knowledge, and experience while experimenting and playing around with ideas. A certain amount of your school day should be dedicated to having discussions that require students to use critical thinking. Examples might include discussions about problems in your community or school, having a topic-of-the-day discussion, or having debates on issues that are of interest to the students. Don't be afraid to say, "I don't know. Let's check into that."

Suggestions for the Teacher

When practicing skills for *Comprehension and Critical Thinking*, it is important to vocalize and discuss the process in finding the answer. After building vocabulary, tapping background knowledge, and discussing the structure that might be used in the article, have the students read each article. If the students are not able to read the article independently, have them read it with another student or in a small teacher-led group. After completing these steps, work through the comprehension questions and the document-based questions. The following are suggestions for working through these activities:

- Have students read the article silently and answer the questions.
- Have students discuss their answers in a small group or with a partner. How did students come up with their answers?
- Have students identify where they were able to locate the answers to the questions.
- Have students analyze the documents that correspond with the articles.
- Have students answer the document-based questions.
- Discuss how students were able to use their prior knowledge in this exercise.

Introduction *(cont.)*

Document-Based Extension Activities: What Are They?

You will notice that some pages in this series are dedicated to providing students with extension document-based activities. These exercises are meant to give your students more experience with analyzing problems or scenarios and using critical thinking skills to solve the problems or offer solutions. You may choose to have the students work through all or some of these activities. You may also opt to have students work independently or in a small group to complete these activities. Sometimes working in a small group is good because it encourages and allows students to see other viewpoints and ideas. Working with other people might also get your students to think "outside the box." Some of the activities lend themselves to independent work and independent thinking. Encourage your students to look for answers that are not typical responses. Teach them how to think further and more critically.

Preparing Students for Standardized Tests

Some of the recent changes taking place in standardized tests have to do with document-based questioning. Along with these document-based questions, students are being asked to write essays on topics generated from documents. Many of our students have little experience writing effective essays. Use the information on the next few pages to help you teach good essay writing skills to your students.

- There are three main parts to an essay. There is the opening paragraph, the middle paragraphs, and the closing paragraph.

- The opening paragraph is meant to hook the reader and to present the topic of the essay. This paragraph will set the reader up for the middle paragraphs.

- The middle paragraphs make up the majority of the essay. Each of the paragraphs in the middle is dedicated to a different point of the essay. These paragraphs are where the evidence and the support are presented. They should be clear and concise.

- The closing paragraph should tie all the important points together. It should restate the point of the essay and should leave the reader with a clear idea of the essay's importance.

Types of Essays

There are different types of essays for different purposes. There are cause/effect essays, problem/solution essays, informative essays, points-of-view essays, and comparison/contrast essays. The type of essay that your students will be writing should be selected before you begin.

Introduction *(cont.)*

Graphic Organizers

Graphic organizers can aid students with comprehension. They can help students comprehend more and, in turn, gain insight into how to comprehend future readings. This process teaches students to connect new information to prior knowledge that is stored in his or her brain. Different types of graphic organizers can be used for different purposes. Graphic organizers can be used to organize information for writing an essay. Here are some examples of graphic organizers that can be used:

Semantic Map—This organizer builds vocabulary. A word for study is placed in the center of the page and four categories are made around it. The categories expand on the nature of the word and relate it back to personal knowledge and experience of the students.

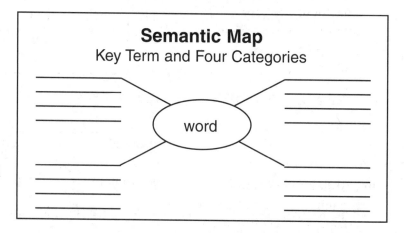

Spider Map (Word Web)—The topic, concept, or theme is placed in the middle of the page. Like a spider's web, thoughts and ideas come out from the center, beginning with main ideas and flowing out to details.

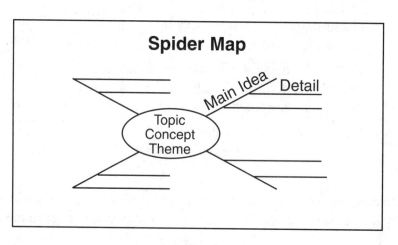

Chain of Events—This organizer not only shows the progression of time but also emphasizes cause and effect. Beginning with the initiating event inside of a box, subsequent arrows and boxes follow showing the events in order.

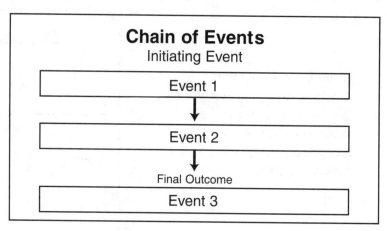

Introduction *(cont.)*

Venn Diagram—This organizer compares and contrasts two ideas. With two large circles intersecting, each circle represents a different topic. The area of each circle that does not intersect is for ideas and concepts that are only true about one topic. The intersection is for ideas and concepts that are true about both topics.

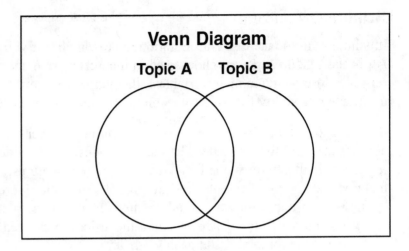

Fishbone Diagram—This organizer deals with cause and effect. The result is listed first, branching out in a fishbone pattern with the causes that lead up to the result, along with other effects that happened along the way.

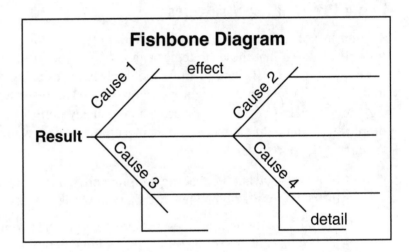

Continuum organizers can be linear or circular and contain a chain of events. These include time lines, chains of events, multiple linear maps, and circular or repeating maps.

Time Lines—Whether graphing ancient history or the last hour, time lines help students to see how events have progressed and to understand patterns in history.

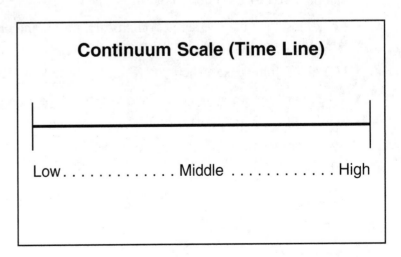

Introduction *(cont.)*

Readability

It is important to take into consideration the readability if you are looking to improve comprehension. All of the *TIME For Kids* articles used in this series have been edited for readability. Readability formulas look at three main variables: the number of words, syllables, and sentences. Most computers now have readability formulas available on the hard drive to determine the readability of a reading text.

Readability formulas are meant to help determine whether a selection of reading material is at the appropriate level for the reader. Readability takes into consideration the book features, the text features, the illustrations, the language and sentence features, and the story features. Each of these features become more complex as the level of readability increases. The number of words on a page, the number of unknown words, and the number of sentences can also affect readability. Through the use of readability formulas, the levels of the articles presented in this series are appropriate and comprehensible for students at each grade level.

Using Pre-reading Strategies

Regular use of pre-reading strategies cannot only help your students comprehend what they are currently reading, but these strategies can also become life-long habits that will aid in comprehension through adulthood. Be sure to stress the importance of using these strategies to your students. Many students lose points on document-based questions and other tests because they don't have the ability to prepare adequately for what they are reading. They don't focus on the details or the directions. Some simple steps can help them develop their patterns of observation. Here are some pre-reading strategies to suggest to your students:

- Know exactly what the reading assignment is, and what you are looking for while you read. Look over the reading assignment. Are there any words you don't know?

- Be familiar with the resources available in your classroom or school library to help you as you read. Some of these resources might include dictionaries, encyclopedias, the Internet, and the index, glossary, etc., in your textbooks.

- Read the titles and headings. Use them to ask yourself questions about what the main idea is and what might be coming up next.

- Try to determine the main idea of each paragraph or chapter. Clearly understanding the main idea can help you focus better on questions later.

- Look closely at maps, graphics, charts, diagrams, and other illustrations to help you understand and remember important information.

- Use all of your senses when you read. What do you picture, hear, smell, etc., while you read?

- Take your time when you come across difficult passages. Reread portions that are unclear or confusing.

Introduction *(cont.)*

Vocabulary Preparation

It is important to prepare your students for vocabulary words that may be new or hard to understand prior to assigning reading. Be sure to read through each of these articles first to be aware of words that might be unknown or difficult for your students to understand. Here are some helpful tips to share with your students when they run across words they don't know:

- Look for comparisons or contrasts used in the sentence.

- Look ahead to see if a definition is included in the sentence.

- Look for other words used in the sentence that might hint at the meaning. For example, there might be synonyms or antonyms used in the sentence that indicate the meaning of a word.

- Look for words in a series. If you know the other words in the series, it might help you figure out the meaning of the word.

- Know what kind of word it is. Is it a verb? a noun? an adjective? Sometimes knowing that it is just a foreign word for the name of something doesn't distract from the meaning of the word.

Building Student Vocabulary

Providing your students with strategies they can use to increase their vocabulary not only helps them with the immediate assignment, but also will enable them to overcome future vocabulary hurdles. Try to incorporate the use of the following vocabulary-building strategies in your classroom:

- **Dictionary/Thesaurus**—Be familiar with a dictionary and know how to use one. When all else fails, look it up in the dictionary! This may seem old-fashioned, but it can save time and energy. A thesaurus is another resource available to students, if they know how to effectively use one.

- **Context Clues**—Use context clues to determine the meaning of a word. All words rely on other words in the sentence to make sense. Good readers use context clues regularly and are aware of the different types.

- **Synonyms and Antonyms**—The study of these related words provides a structure for meaning and is also good practice for learning and building vocabulary.

- **Brainstorming**—The use of graphic organizers to list words and ideas can improve vocabulary. Anticipating the types of words and ideas that will appear in the text will help with fluency of reading as well as comprehension.

- **Word Roots and Origins**—The study of these, as well as affixes, will help students to deduce new words. Students can ask themselves, "Does it look like a word I already know? Can I figure out the meaning in the given context?"

- **Semantic Association**—Students brainstorm a list of words associated with a familiar word, sharing each other's knowledge of vocabulary and discussing less familiar words.

Introduction *(cont.)*

Standardized Tests

Standardized tests have become of great importance in education today. As an educator, you are able to see first-hand the benefits and the tradeoffs of this emphasis on standardized testing. You also are aware that standardized tests do not always paint an accurate picture of what your students know or of their abilities. There are many factors that are not taken into consideration when standardized tests are implemented. Some of these factors include the diversity of our country and the experiences of our students, students who do not speak English fluently and therefore cannot understand the directions, and students who live in at-risk areas and therefore do not receive the experiences necessary to perform well on the tests.

Test Success

With the emphasis on standardized tests, there are some things you can do to help your students find success in test taking. The ability to do well when taking traditional standardized tests for comprehension requires at least three things, as follows:

- a large vocabulary of sight words
- the mastery of certain test-taking skills
- the ability to recognize and control stress

Test-taking Skills

As a teacher you can make a difference in how your students will perform on the standardized tests. You may not change the amount of questions your students get right or wrong, but you can do many things that will better prepare them for the tests. Here are a few suggestions:

- Begin teaching test-taking strategies at the beginning of the year. Teach students to break down the directions and translate them into easy, understandable words. Use this series to show students examples of questions that might appear on the test.

- Explain the importance of having the right attitude about taking tests. Encourage students to have an "I think I can do it" thought as opposed to "There's no use in even trying. It's too hard."

- Show students how to decipher the correct answer from the wrong or "almost" correct answers. Show students how to narrow down the answer when they are debating between answers.

- Demonstrate and practice "test etiquette": no talking, active listening, and following directions. Show students how to work within a time frame and how to budget their allotted time for tests.

- Allow time to discuss what it feels like to take tests. Have a class discussion on test anxiety and suggest ideas for overcoming the stress associated with taking tests. As a class, brainstorm a list of things students can do while they are taking a test to keep them calm and confident.

Introduction *(cont.)*

The Answer Key

The answer key in this book is not like answer keys you may usually use. This is because there are different types of questions being asked. Because many of the questions being asked in this series may be open-ended, or have more than one right answer, there may not be a specific answer for each question. Many of the questions require different answers from each student. Please use the following guidelines to assist you:

- If there is a specific answer requested, then the correct answer is listed.

- If there is more than one answer to a question, but the answers need to follow a specific guideline, then a suggested answer has been provided.

- And finally, some questions may simply be answered, "answers will vary." As the teacher, you will need to determine whether the student has answered the question appropriately or not. Look for higher level thinking skills in the answers your students provide.

Use the answers your students give as a guide to let you know which areas need to be addressed in the classroom to better prepare for tests in the future. You may choose to allow students to analyze each other's questions and not use the answer key at all. Use the following questions as a guide:

- Which of these answers would be the most useful or beneficial?

- What are the strengths and weaknesses of each of these answers?

- What were you thinking as you came to this conclusion?

- What influenced you to come to this conclusion?

- Have you had experience with this type of problem or question before?

- How can your prior knowledge help you figure this out?

- What is your first instinct to this question? After you have had time to think, do you still feel the same way?

Summary

Teachers need to find a way to blend test preparation with the process of learning and discovery. It is important for students to learn test-taking skills and to analyze documents. These skills will be important throughout life. It is also important for students to build vocabulary and knowledge, to create a solid foundation of comprehension skills, and to become fluent readers.

The *Comprehension and Critical Thinking* series is an outstanding program to start your students in the direction of becoming better readers and test-takers. Provide your students with an atmosphere of joy of learning and create a climate for curiosity within your classroom. With daily practice of comprehension and critical thinking skills, as well as test-taking strategies, teaching comprehension may seem just a little bit easier.

Fearless Fashion

You get out of bed, stare into the closet, and ask yourself, "What should I wear to school?" For school students in Long Beach, California, the answer is simple. They put on a school uniform.

The uniforms are navy pants, shorts, or skirts, and white shirts. Most of Long Beach's elementary and middle school students say it's cool to wear uniforms to school. "I don't have to worry about what I wear in the morning," says Sarah Williams, 12. "I just slip on the clothes."

There's something else these Long Beach kids don't have to worry about much anymore: crime at their schools. Long Beach became the nation's first school district in decades to require uniforms. School is a safer place. Crime has dropped. Fighting is down. Student suspensions have decreased.

With uniforms, kids cannot wear colors that connect them to street gangs. "If you don't wear a uniform, they think that you might be a gang member," says Jeff Smart, 11. "With the new uniforms," says Amy Hanson, "my parents don't worry about me getting hurt by bad people."

Uniforms also mean less showing off and less jealousy. Before uniforms, kids compared their jewelry, designer clothes, and high-priced sneakers. "But now," says the vice-principal at Washington Middle School, "there is not as much competition over the way you look."

Before it came up with the dress code, Long Beach did its homework. The school district studied schools that require uniforms in several countries. It found that students who wear uniforms do better in their classes.

Long Beach's success with uniforms has encouraged others. So far, California, Georgia, Florida, Louisiana, Maryland, New York, and Virginia have passed laws that allow public schools to require uniforms.

But not everyone thinks uniforms are a great idea. Some Long Beach parents have sued the school system. They complain that schools require the uniforms but do not help the poor parents pay for them. Some kids dislike dressing the same as everyone else. "I don't like tucking in my shirt," gripes Jason Smith.

Are uniforms a uniformly good idea? How would kids in your school like them?

Fearless Fashion *(cont.)*

Directions: Answer the questions. You may look at the article.

1. Why did the school district make the uniforms mandatory?

2. Describe the uniform that students wear in Long Beach, California.

3. If the students in your school were now required to wear school uniforms, predict what you think their response would be. Why do you think students would react that way?

4. On the back of this paper, illustrate a picture of what you think would be the perfect school uniform. What would students love to wear?

5. Make a list comparing the similarities and the differences between your school and the schools mentioned in the article.

6. Explain the two viewpoints that people might have about uniforms. What are the pros and cons?

7. Rewrite the last paragraph of "Fearless Fashion." Begin the paragraph with the question "Are uniforms a uniformly good idea?" Then go on to express your opinion in paragraph form.

8. Compose a fictional letter to your local school board supporting the creation or elimination of school uniforms. Be sure to support your opinion with examples from the article.

9. Assess how you think uniforms affect the behavior of students. Do they have an effect on the amount of crime, fighting, and suspensions in schools?

Fearless Fashion *(cont.)*

Below is a graph that shows the level of crime, violence, and substance abuse at the Long Beach, California school district. The results of this graph helped the school district decide to make school uniforms mandatory. Use the graph to complete the answers below.

Crime-Stopping Clothes

Since Long Beach, California, started requiring middle and elementary school students to wear uniforms, the number of crimes committed has fallen.

	1993-1994	1994-1995	Percent Change
Assault/Battery	319	212	-34
Fighting	1,135	554	-51
Robbery	29	10	-65
Chemical Substances	71	22	-69
Weapons or Look-Alikes	165	78	-52
Vandalism	1,409	1,155	-18
Dangerous Devices	46	23	-50

Source: Long Beach Unified School District

1. The graph above compares the statistics of violence in schools at Long Beach Unified School District between 1993 and 1995. Look over the statistics. What does the information on this graph tell us? What conclusions can be made about uniforms?

2. Look back at the article, "Fearless Fashion." What did the Long Beach Unified School District look at and research before requiring uniforms? Make a list of these items and use them in your own research of whether or not your school should have uniforms.

3. Imagine you have been asked to survey the students in your school about uniforms. Make a list of questions that you can use to poll the students in your school. How do you think the answers of parents and students would differ on this survey?

Fearless Fashion *(cont.)*

Document-Based Extension Activities

Work independently or in a small group to complete the following.

1. Imagine that your group has been given the assignment to determine whether or not school uniforms would be helpful in your school. Go through the steps to determine the pros and cons of uniforms in your school. Brainstorm as a group what information you would need to determine the necessity of uniforms.

2. Research how uniforms are being used in other schools. Are there any schools requiring uniforms in your town? Any in your state or surrounding states? Interview personnel via e-mail or in person to gather their input on the topic of uniforms.

3. Create a survey that you can use to poll the students in your school. Be sure to survey a large number of students to get an accurate view. Use the same survey to poll the teachers and administrators at your school, as well as a large sample of parents. What are the results?

4. Interview the person in charge of discipline at your school and ask about the crime, violence, and suspension rate at your school. Ask this person his or her opinion on whether or not he or she thinks school uniforms would curb these safety problems.

5. Interview the school administrators to find out what the history of school uniforms has been in this school district. Has anyone attempted to try school uniforms before? What happened and what is the feeling about school uniforms?

6. See if you can set up an interview with a member of the school board. Talk with the school board member about the process to bring the topic of school uniforms to the attention of the school and the school board members. Attend a school board meeting and take notes about how changes are made and accepted in the district.

7. Analyze your findings. Look at the results of your surveys, interviews, observations, and research. Is your school a candidate for required school uniforms? As a group, write a recommendation to your teacher. Be sure to reference your research. Include all of your research and findings with your recommendation.

Crushed by the Quake

People are nervous in Turkey. More than 1,000 small earthquakes shook the land in the weeks after a mighty earthquake struck there on August 17, 1999.

The strongest aftershock hit Turkey two weeks later. "I saw the walls cracking; the cupboard fell in front of me, and I was about to pass out," said a man, who was in his house in the town of Kullar. "I was scared."

The aftershocks, which can continue for up to a month, caused even greater loss in a country that has already lost so much. At least 14,202 people were killed in the first earthquake, and 600,000 lost their homes. Thousands more were missing.

Most people in northwestern Turkey were sleeping when the giant earthquake hit at 3:02 A.M. on August 17. For 45 seconds, the ground shook with a violent rage. "My mom woke me up, and we ran from the building," said a 12-year-old boy. "I thought I was going to die."

When the sun rose that morning, Turkey's heartland lay in ruin. Buildings were smashed into mountains of concrete and steel, with thousands of people trapped underneath them.

The earthquake's center was near the city of Izmit. That is because the city stands atop a huge underground crack, called a fault line. The fault line is more than 600 miles long and 10 miles deep. The rocks alongside it move about an eighth of an inch each year. As they move, they put pressure on nearby rocks. Earthquakes occur when the rocks finally give way.

Immediately after the quake, some families were angry that help did not arrive soon enough. Many were also angry with builders who had used cheap materials. Their buildings had crumbled as easily as sandcastles.

After the quake hit, thousands of Turks lived in tents. With cold weather on the way, the government promised to find houses for quake victims. Said the State Minister of Turkey, "We are not going to let people spend the winter in tents."

Crushed by the Quake *(cont.)*

Directions: Answer the questions. You may look at the article.

1. When and where was the earthquake mentioned in the article?

2. Describe what it would have been like to be in the earthquake in Turkey.

3. Summarize what a fault line is.

4. Draw a picture or diagram of a fault line and how it works.

5. Apply the experience of the earthquake victims to your life. What would frighten you the most about being in an earthquake? What would you do?

6. Locate information about an earthquake that has happened since the earthquake in Turkey. How are these two earthquakes alike and different?

7. Why would people knowingly build on a fault line?

8. What if the earthquake had taken place in the afternoon instead of in the early morning? How would things have been different?

9. Rewrite the second to the last paragraph in the article. Write it as if the rescue teams had arrived quickly to help the earthquake victims.

10. Write a recommendation on what the government in Turkey should do to help its people.

Crushed by the Quake *(cont.)*

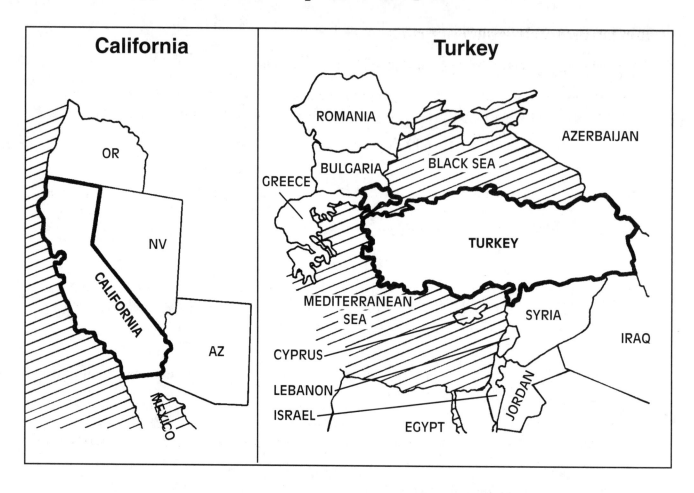

1. Look at the map of Turkey above. Which bodies of water surround Turkey?

2. Look at the map of California. A few years ago, there was an earthquake in California. Using the maps, how are Turkey and the state of California similar and different?

3. What do you think the governments in Turkey and California should do to prepare their citizens for an earthquake?

4. What role do you think governments should play in natural disasters?

Crushed by the Quake *(cont.)*

Document-Based Extension Activities

Work independently or in a small group to complete the following.

1. Why do you think so many people were hurt by the quake? What would it take to be able to prepare for something like that? Have you ever been involved in something so scary and so earth shattering? What was it like? How did you feel?

2. Imagine that you are a child involved in the earthquake. What do you think about the experience? Write a fictional journal entry expressing your thoughts. What do you think should be done to prevent tragedy from earthquakes happening again?

3. The map shows the lands of California and Turkey. Does this map show which cities might be affected most by an earthquake? What other types of information can be gathered from the map that would be helpful to scientists that study earthquakes?

4. Write an essay trying to persuade the U.S. government to take a more active role in protecting the citizens in case of an earthquake. Prior to writing your essay, be sure you have a clear understanding of what your suggestion is. Write your opinion statement. Be sure that it is easy to read and understand. Then make a list of reasons to support your opinion statement. In which order should these ideas be presented?

5. Write a newspaper article about the events of the earthquake and what has happened since. In your article, be sure you answer the following questions: who, what, where, when, why, and how. Type the news article into the computer and select a graphic or photo to accompany your article.

6. Survey the students in your school. Do they know what causes an earthquake? Do they know what to do in case of an earthquake? Do they know first aid and can they help if needed in an emergency? How does education help people live longer and save lives? How does education help us make better choices and prevent tragedy?

7. Write up a proposal that would help the government of Turkey care for its citizens after the earthquake. Look at both sides of the issue before making any suggestions. Be sure that you have looked at all angles. Be sure that your proposal is written as a rough draft and then transfer it to the computer. Typing it up will make it look more professional and official. What do you think the response to your proposal will be?

She's for the Birds

When Anna-Maria Giordano was young she loved birds. She would go to the store to buy birds. They were finches. Finches are small, perky birds. "I started buying singing birds," she says. Anna-Maria always set them free.

Anna-Maria lives in Italy. Millions of birds fly over the island each spring. This is where they lay their eggs. Sadly, a bird set free in Sicily is in danger in the skies. Some people shoot these birds. The birds are storks, honey buzzards, golden orioles, swallows, and quail flying north. Although hunting such birds is not allowed, people do it anyway. Many times the people who shoot the birds never get in trouble.

When Anna-Maria was 15, she decided to help the birds. First, she tried to get forest rangers to catch people that weren't obeying the hunting laws. That went nowhere. "They all made fun of me because I was just 15, and I was trying to tell them what to do."

Anna-Maria and her friend decided they would work together to catch the shooters. They went into the woods every year during April and May to look for people who were shooting the birds. Angry people would yell mean things to Anna-Maria and her friend.

When she was 22, someone set Anna-Maria's car on fire. Most likely it was the hunters. They even mailed her a dead falcon and a note that said, "Your courage will cost you dearly."

Anna-Maria was bothered by the threats, but she wasn't about to quit. In fact, the abuse she suffered from the hunters helped get police officers on her side. "It made the police understand that poaching wasn't just a joke and made them start helping us track down the poachers."

With the help of the police, Anna-Maria has been a big help for the birds that fly over her home. Before she began her work, hunters shot more than 5,000 protected birds each year. Now the number is closer to 200.

Anna-Maria says, "After years of fighting and discussing this problem and writing articles and letters to the newspapers, we have seen the numbers of hunters and slaughtered birds decline each year."

Today, Anna-Maria, is a trained bird scientist. She is trying to raise money to open a center for birds in Italy. The center would teach kids, researchers, and volunteers about bird watching. It would teach people about illegal hunting and environmental protection. It would also have a bird hospital in which injured birds could be treated until their release back into the wild. Meanwhile, she works at a center for injured birds. She is the director of a reserve in Italy. She has won many awards.

She's for the Birds (cont.)

Directions: Answer the questions. You may look at the article.

1. What is Giordano trying to do for the birds?

2. Have Giordano's efforts helped? Before Giordano started her patrol, 5,000 birds were shot each year. About how many birds are shot now?

3. What are the different things Giordano does to protect the birds? What do you predict will happen if Giordano continues her efforts?

4. Describe what some people have done to try and scare Giordano from her work.

5. Describe how Giordano was able to change public opinion about the shooting of protected birds.

6. Illustrate a picture that Giordano could use to encourage others to protect the birds.

7. In the article, it states that in time Giordano gained support from local law enforcement officers. Explain how this gives Giordano added support for her efforts.

8. Make a list of things Giordano does to successfully save the birds.

9. Summarize the characteristics of Giordano's personality that make her successful.

She's for the Birds *(cont.)*

Giordano is a member of the World Wildlife Fund Center for the Rehabilitation of Injured Birds in Messina. There are companies that are in support of what the World Wildlife Fund is trying to accomplish. Look at the fictional letter from a fictional shoe company to the World Wildlife Fund.

World Wildlife Fund
Via Filippo Turati 33
00185-Messina
Italy

Dear World Wildlife Fund,

Run for Life, Inc. would like to express our support of your environmental changes. Please see the list of agreements we would be willing to make with the World Wildlife Fund. Under the new agreement, World Wildlife Fund and *Run for Life, Inc.* will work to achieve the following climate-saving targets:

- Reduce carbon dioxide emissions from business travel and *Run for Life, Inc.* owned facilities. *Run for Life, Inc.* intends to reduce and/or eliminate greenhouse gas emissions, within the next ten years.

- Create shoes and other products that use recycled materials. It is our belief that recycled materials can not only provide high quality products, but can improve wildlife and natural climates.

- Examine *Run for Life, Inc.'s* means of packaging and transportation to improve pollution levels in the cities where our company is based.

Please send me a response in agreement or disagreement to these criteria.

Sincerely,

David Baker, CEO
Run for Life, Inc.

---

1. Based on this letter, what do you think is the main goal and purpose of the World Wildlife Fund?

2. What do you think greenhouse gases are? How can you find out?

3. What do you think the letter from the World Wildlife Fund will say to David Baker of *Run for Life, Inc.*? Explain your answer.

4. What other types of projects do you think would interest Anna-Maria? Make a list of these projects and explain your reasons for each.

She's for the Birds (cont.)

Document-Based Extension Activities

Work independently or in a small group to complete the following.

1. How does the letter like the one you just read help support Giordano's cause? How does support from others help send a message? How can a voice of support sometimes send a stronger message than the original work? How can you use this information in the future?

2. Write a cause-and-effect essay on the hunting of birds in Italy. Some things to consider for your essay:

   - Clearly state the cause of the birds being shot.
   - What are the effects of these causes?
   - Suggested wording for cause-and-effect essays include: Because of . . . we now; When . . . happened, I . . .
   - What can alter the cause and effect?

3. How can you become involved in an issue that is going on half way around the world? How can you help from such a distance? Brainstorm with a partner a list of things that can be done to help the rain forest. Share your list with the class. See if they have more to add to it.

4. Kids have raised money for many different causes. Some kids have raised money to save the environment, or to save whales, etc. How does money help these causes? Would money help save the birds in Italy? How?

5. Research on the Internet, or use other sources, to find out why people are killing the birds. What would be the benefits of killing the birds? Make a list of the reasons why people kill the birds.

6. What suggestions do you have as punishment for people that shoot the birds? Compare your answers with another student. Are your answers similar or different? Which do you think would be the most successful? Which would be the easiest to carry out?

The Packs Are Back

For many years, gray wolves lived in the forests of the American West. They had few enemies. Then, in the early 1800s, people began to arrive. People were afraid of these wild, sharp-toothed creatures. Wolves sometimes killed farmers' animals. People worried that they might attack humans, too.

Some wolves were shot. The government paid hunters a reward for each wolf they killed. By the early 1930s, no wolves were left in Yellowstone National Park. The disappearance of wolves left a big hole in Yellowstone's ecosystem. Coyotes became too numerous. Foxes and badgers, which eat the same little animals that coyotes do, were going hungry. The ecosystem was badly out of balance.

To fix the problem in Yellowstone, the U.S. Fish and Wildlife Service decided to bring back wolves. In 1995, 31 gray wolves from Canada were brought to the park. Since then, something incredible has happened: Yellowstone has come howling back to life.

Grizzly bears are no longer forced to strip the trees of nuts and leaves because they can eat the wolves' leftovers. There are fewer coyotes. That means there are more little animals for the foxes, badgers, and eagles to eat.

Even trees and plants are healthier now that bears and elk don't snack on them as much. These changes in Yellowstone show that the return of the wolves has been a good thing. "Ecological change seldom happens before your eyes," says John Valley, a director at Yellowstone National Park. "I never imagined we'd see it."

Some people don't like the changes, however. Ranchers near the park still want to get rid of their old enemy.

Since 1995, wolves have killed 84 sheep and seven cattle. A group has paid the ranchers to replace the animals. But the ranchers complain that they never know when a wolf will strike.

Vern Keller and others went to court. They argued that the way in which Yellowstone's new wolves were brought into the park was not legal. In December 1997, a judge agreed and ordered the wolves to be removed. Environmental groups are fighting the decision.

The original 31 animals have multiplied to between 150 and 200. They cannot be shipped back to Canada because their old territory has been taken over by other wolves. Zoos aren't likely to take them. Yellowstone scientist Douglas Smith says, "The options could come down to killing them."

The judge's decision is still being appealed. In fact, the case may go all the way to the Supreme Court. "I will fight with everything I have to keep the wolves in Yellowstone," said one man.

The wolves are used to being the focus of a fight. It's been that way for many years. However, humans must not let the wolves leave the park.

The Packs are Back (cont.)

Directions: Answer the questions. You may look at the article.

1. Why are people afraid of the wolves?

2. In what year did Yellowstone Park receive wolves again? Why were they brought back?

3. Predict what the ranchers will do if the wolves are allowed in Yellowstone.

4. Why do you think the ranchers are opposed to the wolves even though they are compensated for any animals killed by the wolves?

5. Compare the pros and cons of the wolves being in Yellowstone.

6. Explain how the ecosystem improved in Yellowstone when the wolves were returned.

7. What can farmers do to protect their flocks from the wolves in Yellowstone?

8. What is the author's opinion of the wolves? What statements give you an idea of his or her opinion?

9. Based on the information in the article, would you recommend that the wolves be allowed in Yellowstone? Explain your answer.

The Packs are Back *(cont.)*

The debate about the wolves in Yellowstone National Park is ongoing. Here is a political cartoon on the subject. Base your answers to the following questions on the cartoon below, as well as your knowledge of the debate about wolves in Yellowstone.

1. What stories are being referred to in this cartoon?

2. What is the message of the cartoon?

3. Do you think the return of wolves to Yellowstone National Park is a positive or negative step? Explain your answer.

4. How would this cartoon be changed if it were written by someone with the opposing view?

The Packs are Back *(cont.)*

Document-Based Extension Activities

Work independently or in a small group to complete the following.

1. Analyze the scenario with the wolves and the ranchers in Yellowstone, and write a plan of resolution. Then analyze how you think both individuals involved in the plan are going to react. How will they feel about your proposed solution? Have you addressed all the issues? Have you ignored the intent of some of the individuals? Are you taking sides? Type up your plan and have it analyzed by another classmate before you turn it in.

2. How are conflicts resolved in your community? Do you agree with the way conflicts or disagreements are addressed in your school? Draft a list of questions that can be asked of fellow students about the discipline in your school. Some questions might include the following:

   - Are students respected for their different beliefs on issues?
   - Do you think that disagreements and conflicts are handled appropriately in our school?
   - Do the students respect the teachers and other adults at our school?
   - Do you think that students are learning conflict resolution skills in our school?

3. Analyze the results of the survey. What do the students at your school think about differences of opinion? Do they feel safe? Do they feel like issues are under control? Do they feel like they can freely express their opinion? What issues are not being addressed? Brainstorm a list of possible solutions or plans to address these weak areas.

4. Keep a log of incidents that would require compromise or respect for differences at your school. Categorize the incidents into different categories based on the type and seriousness of the incidents. Assess whether or not you think that the students in your school need to learn how to respect differences of opinion.

5. Look for examples in the newspaper of two sides not in agreement like the ranchers and the supporters of wolves in Yellowstone. How are these cases similar or different?

6. Draft a letter to one of the groups involved with the issue of wolves in Yellowstone. Share with the group an analysis you've done of the issue, the results of the survey of students, and your recommendations. Design letterhead on the computer and type your letter on it. Be sure to check the spelling and grammar in your letter. It needs to look professional in order for the letter to be taken seriously.

Green Thumbs

I griped and moaned the whole day. My parents were making me work on the neighborhood project, and I had better things to do. It was just the ugly, old, vacant lot across from Johnny's Shop and Go. It was full of weeds, greasy fast food wrappers, old newspapers, broken glass, and every other kind of nasty trash you can imagine. As I looked at it that first morning, I thought, "I bet there are snakes in there, too." I would rather have been anywhere else.

There were twenty of us—all ages and sizes—ready to work that day. The idea that this awful mess could be cleaned, let alone made into a garden showplace, seemed unlikely. I suspect we were all wondering where to begin. Then Mr. Hernandez said, "The only way to do it is just to start." Then he divided the lot into fourths with string and assigned five people to each quadrant.

By lunchtime, I was hot, sweaty, grimy, and glad my dad had made me wear gloves. (The rusty cans and shards of glass were wicked!) We had filled fifty trash bags with junk and were ready to pull weeds. Great! Now it was time to get a nose-full of pollen and go into an allergic sneeze-fest. Did you know that weeds can make you itch?

At the end of the day, I had to admit the lot looked better. Bare, but better. My dad was starting to till the dirt. A tiller is a weird-looking machine that a person holds onto by two handles. It's kind of a personal-size tractor that you manage like a lawn mower. It has a gas motor that drives these rotating blades and pushes it along. The blades lift and turn the dirt and get it ready to plant. Watching Dad's shoulders strain and his arms jostle, I thought how he and the tiller seemed a team—like a farmer driving his mechanical, earth-eating mule.

That first day was the toughest. In the weekends that followed, we made rows, planted flower and vegetable seeds, fertilized, watered, and weeded. After about two weeks, I stopped griping. The plants had started popping up! First the lettuce, then the beans and squash. They grew so fast, I couldn't believe it! Some days, a bean plant would grow an inch. A zucchini leaf could double in size in just a few days.

Now, two months later, I like to go there every day to see what new flowers are ready to pop. The marigolds are my favorites with their fat, rich, orange blooms. Lots of people in the neighborhood meet there to enjoy the sights and talk. Tonight, it suddenly hit me—what a good thing we did! I'm proud I have been a part of it. The vegetables will go to the food pantry. I'm in charge of picking bouquets for the nursing home on Fourth Avenue. But even better, an eyesore that people avoided has become a pretty patch of green—a place for everyone to enjoy.

Green Thumbs (cont.)

Directions: Answer the questions. You may look at the article.

1. What was the neighborhood project? How many people were involved?

2. What did Mr. Hernandez do to get the project organized and started?

3. How did the author feel about the neighborhood project? Make a list of words that show you how the author feels.

4. Describe what it would have felt like to work on the neighborhood project.

5. Draw a time line with small pictures showing the progress of the neighborhood project. Is there a project in your neighborhood waiting to be done?

6. Obviously this neighborhood project was successful. List the reasons why you think it ended up being a positive project and experience.

7. What if the author never changed his attitude about the neighborhood project? How might the article be different?

8. Prepare a plan for a project that can be done to improve your neighborhood. Make a list of steps to follow and the materials that will be needed.

9. What could you say to convince your neighbors to participate in your project? Write a letter to convince your neighbors.

Green Thumbs (cont.)

The members of the neighborhood mentioned in the article worked hard to improve their surroundings. This sign was posted days after the project was complete. Use the sign to answer the questions at the bottom of the page.

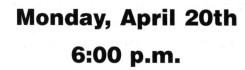

You are invited to attend the...

First Annual Neighborhood Party!

Monday, April 20th

6:00 p.m.

~ Potluck Dinner ~

Please bring a dish to share.

Napkins, forks, plates, and cups will be provided.

Let's meet in the newly remodeled vacant lot.

Bring plans for future neighborhood projects!

1. What is this sign advertising? Do you think this event being advertised will be successful? What evidence do you have for this?

2. How do you think the people of the neighborhood are feeling about their work on the vacant lot, as well as their relationships with each other?

3. Give three examples of what the people in this neighborhood have done or are planning to do together.

4. Explain the steps that the people of the neighborhood followed to find success in both improving their neighborhood and their relationships.

Green Thumbs *(cont.)*

Document-Based Extension Activities

Work independently or in a small group to complete the following.

1. Use your prior knowledge, and the knowledge you gained from reading the article and the invitation to the neighborhood party. Brainstorm a list of projects that you could do in your neighborhood. As you make the list, write down the pros and cons, the materials needed, and the feasibility of each project.

2. Design an informational pamphlet or brochure inviting members of your own neighborhood to join in on the project. Type the pamphlet into the computer. Be sure to format the pamphlet on the horizontal option for the paper. Then you can fold the paper into thirds to make it look like a pamphlet. You will need to spotlight certain information by putting it in larger, bold-faced letters and by using pictures and call-outs to get your point across. The computer will lend itself to graphics and clip art.

3. Write a plan to fulfill your neighborhood project. Read through the article again to clarify the problems and brainstorm other things that might keep the project from being successful. Try to keep in mind the attitude of the group. At first, the author of the article wasn't sure the project was a good idea and had a bad attitude. But given some time, he was able to come around. Anticipate these problems, so you can respond to them. For each anticipated problem, think up a solution to correct or prevent the problem. Submit your plan to a parent. Ask him or her to read the plan and give you feedback. Using the feedback, alter or rewrite your plan accordingly.

4. Locate and gather maps of your community. Research and gather information about rules and restrictions. Are there laws that need to be taken into consideration? Create a map showing the exact location of the project. Write a letter to community leaders, requesting permission to complete your project. Send the letter, if so desired.

5. As humans, we try to make a difference. With some planning and help from some friends you might be able to do the same thing. Set up a time, date, and schedule for people to follow regarding the neighborhood project. Take before and after pictures. Invite the local newspaper to come and document the project. Review your project on completion. Did you follow the plan? What did you learn from this experience? Write an essay about the choices that we make and how they affect others. In your essay, make a suggestion of steps to follow prior to making serious decisions that can affect others.

Another Star on Our Flag

The Caribbean Island of Puerto Rico has been a part of the U.S. for years. Many Americans don't even realize that Puerto Rico's residents are U.S. citizens. They are, but Puerto Rico's residents do not pay federal income taxes. They cannot vote for president of the U.S. or for Congress.

Puerto Rico has a governor and a delegate to the U.S. Congress, but that person has no vote. The island is a commonwealth. Puerto Rico is a self-governing part of the U.S., but not a state. Puerto Ricans should vote to become the 51st American State.

The relationship between the U.S. and Puerto Rico would be easier if Puerto Rico became a state. Its governor agrees. "It is not okay to keep nearly 4 million U.S. citizens without their full citizenship rights," says Governor Pedro Russell.

In 1998, the island's voters went to the polls. They voted on whether or not they wanted to become a state. In the election, 46% voted for statehood. Fifty percent of the voters voted "none of the above." Governor Russell sees the vote as support for statehood, saying that "none of the above" was not a valid choice. However, for now, Puerto Rico will continue as a commonwealth.

Puerto Rico is 900 miles southeast of Miami. Christopher Columbus discovered it in 1493. Spain ruled it for 400 years. It became a U.S. possession at the end of the Spanish-American War in 1898. Today, Puerto Ricans are divided over the island's political relationship to the U.S.

Historically, many Puerto Ricans want to remain a commonwealth. "Puerto Ricans want to have ties to the U.S. They also want to protect their culture and language," says Roberto Prates, 32, a lawyer in San Juan. "The only status that guarantees this is the commonwealth." Some people fear that if the island becomes a state, it may lose its unique identity. These people should look to Hawaii, our 50th state. Not only has Hawaii kept its unique culture, but other Americans have enjoyed learning about it and experiencing it, as well.

Some Puerto Ricans don't like statehood because they do not want to pay more taxes. But many citizens are willing to pay U.S. taxes in order to be a part of the booming U.S. economy. Already, two million Puerto Ricans live in the U.S. They obviously like the American way of life. Governor Russell thinks support for statehood is growing: "The younger generations are coming in. They're more supportive." If Puerto Ricans someday vote for statehood, the U.S. Congress must then approve a statehood plan. Puerto Ricans should vote in favor of their island becoming the 51st state.

Another Star on Our Flag *(cont.)*

Directions: Answer the questions. You may look at the article.

1. How does the governor of Puerto Rico feel about statehood?

2. Where is Puerto Rico located? When was it discovered? By whom?

3. What was the percentage of people that voted for Puerto Rico statehood? What does that information tell you?

4. Some Puerto Ricans are afraid they would lose their culture and identity if they became the 51st state. Spanish is their main language. Examine the effect becoming a state would have on the language used in Puerto Rico.

5. What are the benefits that the United States would receive from Puerto Rico becoming a state? What are the benefits for Puerto Rico?

6. The last paragraph says two million Puerto Ricans live in the United States. Why would these people want to leave Puerto Rico for the United States?

7. What if you were a citizen of Puerto Rico? Would you support statehood? Why or why not?

8. Design a statehood plan for Puerto Rico to become the 51st state in the United States.

9. What do you think the author's view on this topic is? Was the author of this article convincing? Examine the article. Were the quotes supportive? Was there enough information to support his or her view?

Another Star on Our Flag *(cont.)*

The map below is of Puerto Rico and surrounding countries. This map can help in your analysis as to whether or not Puerto Rico should become a state of the United States.

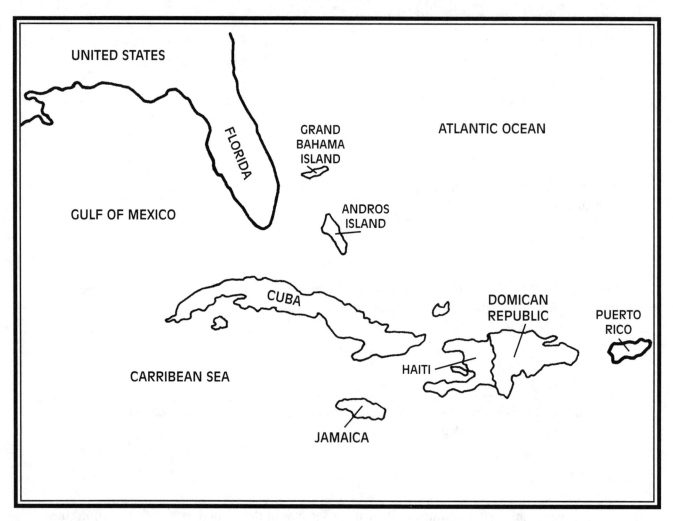

1. Give directions on how someone from the United States would get to Puerto Rico.

2. Using the map as a guide, what would be the benefits of having Puerto Rico as the 51st state of the United States?

3. Again, using the map, what would make it difficult to have Puerto Rico as another state?

4. Puerto Rico is near many islands that are not governed by the United States. Therefore, Puerto Rico should not be a state. Do you agree or disagree? Why?

5. Based on your analysis, write a recommendation to the president of the United States as to whether or not you think Puerto Rico should be granted statehood. Be sure to support your recommendation.

Another Star on Our Flag *(cont.)*

Document-Based Extension Activities

Work independently or in a small group to complete the following.

1. Summarize the two main points of the Puerto Rico debate. List the options that each group can exercise in order to get their wish passed. As a third party, what would you suggest to both sides? Is there room for compromise? Is it possible to compromise on this issue?

2. Using the Internet, research the topic of Puerto Rico becoming a state. Find articles and evidence supporting both sides. Discuss with a small group of students both sides of the issue. Some points/questions to consider for your discussion might be:

   - Clarify the viewpoints on both sides of the issue.
   - What evidence is there to support each side?
   - Who do you think has a stronger case?
   - What are some options that could be considered for a compromise?
   - Do you think a compromise can happen?

3. Write an essay on the viewpoint you think has the strongest case. Be sure to clearly state your opinion and to support it with evidence.

4. There have been other times that Puerto Rico has tried for statehood. What happened in the past? How did Alaska and Hawaii receive their statehood? Was it a similar circumstance? Research these other states. How can the information from these different cases help solve the issue at hand with Puerto Rico? How are things similar or different?

It's Time to Pay the Price

To the Editors:

I am an eighth-grade student at Falcon Middle School. I am upset over the way our teachers are paid. In my opinion, teachers perform one of the most important jobs. They are in charge of teaching us. They are in charge of preparing us for the future. The teachers I know work very hard at that.

We don't pay teachers enough for the very important jobs they do. The average salary for teachers in our area is $29,000. As professionals, teachers should be paid like other professionals, such as lawyers and doctors.

Of course, the question isn't, "Why would anyone want to be a teacher?" The real question is "How could anyone afford to be a teacher when they are paid such a low salary?"

Let me tell you about my social studies teacher, Mrs. Miller. She is an excellent teacher. She spends her own money on projects for her students. She volunteers her free time on weekends. She does this even though she is also raising three kids. Don't you think Mrs. Miller and other teachers like her deserve to be rewarded?

I checked and found out that the low salaries for teachers are not a problem only in our area. It's happening all over the U.S. Teachers' salaries actually went down in 1998.

In order to keep up with the growing number of students, schools need to hire more teachers. There are many teachers retiring. Schools will need to hire over one million new teachers in the next ten years. Do school boards believe they will be able to get one million of the best minds if they are offering such low salaries?

What is the solution? It's simple: raise the salaries of teachers. Make the amount they earn more in line with other professionals.

Sincerely,

Bill Hunter

It's Time to Pay the Price (cont.)

Directions: Answer the questions. You may look at the article.

1. Who does the author think should make more money? Why?

2. Describe in your own words what Mrs. Miller does to be a good teacher.

3. List the reasons the author offers as to why teachers should make more money.

4. Why is it significant that the author brings up the point about needing to hire over one million teachers in the next ten years?

5. Evaluate the title of the article/letter. Does the title fit? What message does the author send by using this title?

6. What ideas can you add to the author's for reasons to pay teachers more?

7. What solutions would you suggest for fixing the teacher shortage?

8. Do you agree with the author? Explain your answer.

It's Time to Pay the Price *(cont.)*

Here is a chart showing the average salaries of teachers in Wisconsin. This chart shows the years of 1985 through 1997. Use this chart to help you answer the questions below.

Average Teacher Salaries in Wisconsin	
Year	**Average Salary**
1985-86	$ 26,347
1986-87	$ 27,815
1987-88	$ 29,122
1988-89	$ 30,779
1989-90	$ 31,921
1990-91	$ 33,209
1991-92	$ 35,227
1992-93	$ 35,926
1993-94	$ 35,990
1994-95	$ 37,746
1995-96	$ 38,182
1996-97	$ 38,950

1. What was the average teacher salary in the year 1991-1992? 1996-97?

2. What do you predict the salaries of teachers to do? Increase? Decrease? Explain your answer.

3. Do you think the state of Wisconsin is able to attract teachers to work there based on their salary history? Explain your answer.

4. Compared to other professionals, teacher salaries are lower. Why do you think teacher salaries are so low compared to other professionals? What suggestions do you have for school districts to pay their teachers more money?

It's Time to Pay the Price (cont.)

Document-Based Extension Activities

Work independently or in a small group to complete the following.

1. Looking at the chart on the previous page, what assumptions can be made about the salary of teachers in Wisconsin? What suggestions do you have for the state to increase the salary of teachers?

2. Research the salaries of teachers in other states. Are the salaries similar or are they different? What can be some of the reasons for the similarities or differences? How are teacher salaries determined? Across the nation, are teacher salaries going up or down? Why?

3. Design a brochure that can be given to parents and government officials to help educate them on the importance of teacher salaries. Use the computer to design the brochure. If you print the brochure horizontally, you can fold the paper into thirds to create the look of a real brochure.

4. Write a letter to the editor of your local paper, discussing the importance of raising teacher salaries. Use evidence you have gathered on teacher salaries across the nation. Type this letter on letterhead you have designed. Send the letter to the local newspaper and see if it is printed.

5. Write a cause-and-effect essay on what will happen if teacher salaries remain low.

6. Look back at the chart. What do you think was going on in the years that teacher salaries were at their lowest? What can states do to increase teacher salaries? What options can you suggest?

A Carousel of Dreams

A new carousel spins around at Riverbank State Park in New York City. But it doesn't hold the usual painted ponies. Instead, giant spiders pull a chariot. A plaid zebra prances beside a two-headed octopus.

These creatures were invented by kids from Harlem and turned into a carousel by Milo Mottola, 32.

Milo was picked in 1993 to plan a carousel for the park. He decided to ask the neighborhood for creative ideas. "I knew that the kids should be part of the job," he says.

Milo held drawing classes in the park. He dressed up as a knight. He taught the kids that carousels come from the medieval times.

"He was very funny," says Ramona Cairo. Ramona's octopus was chosen. There were 32 animals and two chariots chosen for the carousel.

Milo says it was tough to choose the drawings. There were over 1,000 drawings. Milo said, "They were all my favorites!" The original drawings hang above each animal. The signature of the artist is carved on the floor beneath.

While Milo worked on flamingos, kangaroos, and other animals, the kids couldn't wait for the carousel to be done. Grover Austin, whose green lion is in the carousel said, "I'd like to ride it all summer long."

A Carousel of Dreams *(cont.)*

Directions: Answer the questions. You may look at the article.

1. What makes this carousel different than a typical carousel?

2. Who was picked to design the carousel? Who picked the designers? Where is the carousel located?

3. Describe this carousel. What does it look like?

4. How did the children feel about being involved with this project? How can you tell?

5. Explain the process Milo Mottola used to create the carousel. Where are the original drawings posted?

6. How many animals are on this carousel? What other objects were used?

7. What might happen if you combined a medieval theme with a futuristic theme for a carousel?

8. How would you design a carousel of your own? What would it look like? How would it work?

9. What criteria would you use to assess how successful your carousel is? What criteria would you use to assess how successful Mottola's carousel is?

A Carousel of Dreams (cont.)

In response to an article printed in the newspaper about the Carousel of Dreams opening up at Riverbank State Park, this letter to the editor was printed. Read the letter below and answer the questions that follow.

Dear Editor:

After reading the newspaper article on the new carousel opening up at Riverbank State Park in New York City, I thought I would go and check it out. Wow! I was amazed.

Your article mentioned that the children had designed the creatures and the animals on this carousel. I was expecting to see a bunch of messy creatures and dripping paint. Boy, was I mistaken! The carousel is professionally done, with the artwork of the children being the main focus and attraction.

Kudos to Mr. Milo Mottola! He was able to involve our young citizens in improving and enhancing our community. His efforts should be duplicated. We should have more projects that highlight children in our community. I think this would give kids a feeling of ownership in the community to which they belong. This might help curb the problems we have with teenagers vandalizing and littering our towns.

Think about it!

Sincerely,

Frank Johnson

1. What was Mr. Johnson's first impression of the idea of a carousel being designed by kids? Is this a common first impression when it comes to kids doing things?

2. How does Mr. Johnson feel about the Carousel of Dreams? List examples from the letter.

3. What does Mr. Johnson suggest that city and community leaders do to curb vandalism? Do you think it will work? Explain your answer.

4. Imagine that you are Mr. Milo Mottola, the designer of the carousel. Write a fictional letter in response to Mr. Johnson's letter to the editor.

A Carousel of Dreams (cont.)

Document-Based Extension Activities

Work independently or in a small group to complete the following.

1. Draw a diagram of an animal you would put on the carousel. How does it look? What are the parts? Design your animal for the carousel and remember that carousels came from medieval times. Do you think your picture would pass?

2. Pretend you are a news reporter from New York. You are here to do a write-up on the new carousel in town. What would you find? What would you think? What is the carousel like? What do people have to look forward to?

3. Using your prior knowledge, design a brochure that spotlights the Carousel of Dreams. You can make a brochure by folding a horizontal piece of paper into thirds. You will need to spotlight certain information by putting it in larger, bold-faced letters and by using pictures to get your point across. This can be done using the computer. The computer will lend itself to graphics as well as clip art.

4. Read through the article again to determine how this carousel came about. Write a plan to design something in the public park in your community. For each problem, think up a solution to correct or prevent the problem. Submit your plan to a local governing body for review. Ask them to read the plan and give you feedback. Using the feedback, alter or rewrite part of your plan.

5. Locate and gather advice from different groups in the community as to what kind of park project you should do. Take a poll to find out the interests and the history of the community. Can you tie these ideas together?

6. Write an essay about the pros and cons of putting together a new project in the public park. Some people may not agree with you. Be sure to support both sides of the issue. An essay needs evidence to support the idea. You may choose to write the essay about only the pros or only the cons. Or, you may choose to write your essay about both the pros and the cons. Be sure that you have accurate information to present as evidence.

Into the Dark Unknown

Some days Louise Hose puts on a suit to go to work. Other days she braids her long, blond hair and puts on a helmet with a large headlamp. Sometimes she even wears a gas mask and kneepads. When she isn't dressed up to teach geology courses at a college, Hose is exploring and mapping caves. She likes caves that are deep and dark.

Hose is a geologist and a speleologist, or caver. Her job is to add to our knowledge about how the earth is formed. Sometimes she crawls on her back through tight passages with rocks pressing into her body. Other times she dangles on the end of a secured rope, down the wall of a deep cave.

For the past few years, she has gone to Tapijulapa, Mexico, during school breaks to map a cave. She and her fellow explorers have found that it is full of animals that have adapted to life underground. There are vampire bats, spiders, and colorless fish and crabs that swim in the cave's streams.

They also discovered something more amazing—colonies of microscopic living creatures that can survive in poisonous air and with no light. Such creatures may give clues to what life forms are like in space. These living colonies drip down like a runny nose. They contain sulfuric acid, which can burn human skin. A photographer on the expedition named the slimy critters "snottites."

"Caves are one of the last parts of the earth that aren't mapped yet," says Hose. "It's true exploring." She likes going through the unknown. "When you are the first person to explore a cave, you don't know what you are going to find," she says. Sometimes she finds minerals that shimmer in her headlamp.

When Hose was a kid in Alhambra, California, she loved to watch adventure shows. But the brave explorers she saw were always men. "I used to wish I was a boy, so I could be an explorer," she recalls. "Thank goodness I studied geology." Her studies gave her confidence to discover new things. She said, "Girls can and do become explorers."

Into the Dark Unknown (cont.)

Directions: Answer the questions. You may look at the article.

1. What is a speleologist? What is the job of a geologist and speleologist?

2. What is unique about the cave Hose is exploring in Tapijulapa, Mexico?

3. Describe how Louise Hose feels about exploring caves.

4. How does the cave in Tapijulapa, Mexico, compare and contrast with other caves?

5. How is Hose a role model for young girls interested in adventure?

6. Explain why the findings of the microscopic creatures surviving in poisonous air and no light are so amazing.

7. What if Louise Hose believed that only men could be explorers? What are some of your goals?

8. What message do you think the author is trying to send? Is the message about exploring caves or fulfilling your dreams?

9. What criteria would you use to assess whether or not Louise Hose is successful? Explain your opinion of her success.

Into the Dark Unknown *(cont.)*

When is the last time that you stepped foot inside a cave? Caving can be an exciting adventure. Look at the picture below and use it to answer the questions that follow.

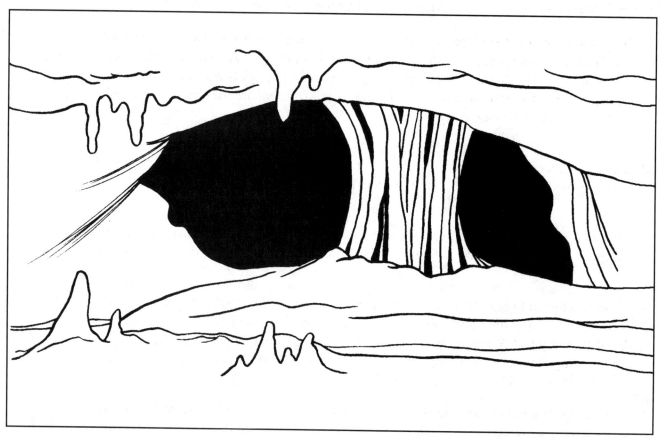

1. What is the picture above?

2. What types of dangers would you have to think about before entering the cave?

3. What types of tools would you find helpful in exploring this cave?

4. Write a paragraph describing an imaginary experience you had going inside this cave.

Into the Dark Unknown (cont.)

Document-Based Extension Activities

Work independently or in a small group to complete the following.

1. Take a survey of the students in your class, as well as an older group such as parents, teachers, neighbors, or grandparents. Ask them to list careers for girls. Analyze the responses. What did you find out? Do all people have the same expectations for girls and their careers? Does age make a difference on what people think girls can do? What are the reasons why girls are not expected to go into some careers?

2. Have you ever been in a cave? Write about that experience. What did you see? hear? smell? feel? How is being in a cave different than being above ground?

3. In the article it mentioned that some animals have adapted to living underground. Why is this so unique? Why do you think animals would choose to live underground?

4. Write a letter to Louise Hose and ask her questions about the variety of jobs that she does. Which job does she enjoy the most? Why does she do more than one job? What has she learned from her different jobs? What are her plans for the future? What advice does she have for girls? Type up the imaginary letter and design your own letterhead. Share the letters as a class.

5. Gather information on a group of caves in the United States or other countries. Identify five of these caves. Research as much information as you can find on these caves. Compare and contrast the five caves—including the cave in Tapijulapa, Mexico. How are these caves alike? How are these caves different? Which cave do you find most interesting? Why?

6. What can the media do to encourage young girls to go after their dreams? How do you think the media can discourage or encourage girls? How much of an influence do you think the media has on girls?

7. Make a list of goals and plans that you have for the future. Under each goal, write down the steps that you plan to take in order to accomplish these goals. What needs to be done now? In one year? In five years? Make a list of people that can assist you in accomplishing these goals. Be sure to set up a strong support system to help you accomplish these goals. Keep a journal to record your experiences and ideas.

8. Write a letter to yourself that you will open in five years. What do you wish to be doing in five years? What do you want to remember in five years? Seal the letter in an envelope and keep it in a safe place so that you will be able to find it.

Accident Prone

The old man walked slowly in front of us. With a smile, he raised his gun and fired. A roar exploded from the crowd of 220 as we rushed toward him. The man moved quickly, trying to get out of the way. He stumbled and just barely managed to gain safety as we raced past him. The High School Cross Country Championship had begun. Pumping my legs, I pushed myself harder than I normally did at the start of a 5K race. For a brief moment, I led the pack. Only the winding, painted path stretched before me as it snaked toward the woods. A blur of movement appeared next to me.

Without looking, I knew it was Noel. "Hey, Cliff," Noel said. "How's the leg?" Ignore him and keep running, I told myself. But I couldn't stop the twinge of pain in my leg—a reminder of what happened two years ago . . .

We had been racing on this same course. Once the woods had hidden us from spectators, Noel had dragged his spiked shoe down the back of my right leg. The little spikes had felt like sharp fangs digging into my calf. I had tried to keep running, but it hurt too much. I had to stop while Noel zipped ahead to victory. Later, Noel insisted that the whole thing had been an accident and that he was sorry. I didn't believe any of it—accidents like that don't happen. Now, here we were again: the two of us in the lead, heading for the woods. Noel turned his head toward me and said, "Listen, I want to apologize." To cut him off, I added a burst of speed to my stride, but he matched my exertion.

Then we were in the forest. Trees formed thick walls along the path. The other runners were seconds behind – it was just the two of us. He's going to do it again, I thought. He's going to use the bottom of his shoe to put himself on top! "Keep your distance," I told him.

"Hey, you have the wrong idea about me," Noel said. The trees crowded the path, narrowing the course. Noel swerved, closing the gap between us. I jerked to the side, trying to avoid him. Ahead, I could see the light of day. In about 100 yards, the path would take us out of the woods. "Almost there," I thought.

And then I tripped. I had been so busy trying to keep track of Noel that I failed to notice an orange construction barrel used by race officials to mark the course. My foot caught the rounded edge of the barrel, and I fell, crashing to the ground. I looked up expecting to see Noel's body getting smaller and smaller as he headed toward the finish line and the first place trophy. But instead, I saw a hand directly in front of my face. It belonged to Noel.

"Get up," he said to me, putting his hand out farther. I hesitated, and he shouted, "Hurry!" I grabbed his hand and he helped me to my feet. "Now, let's run a real race," Noel said with a grin. With that we were off, racing toward the finish line. But not before I noticed what my collision with the barrel had caused. Scratch lines from my spiked shoes marred the barrel's orange surface. I guess accidents do happen.

Accident Prone (cont.)

Directions: Answer the questions. You may look at the article.

1. Who is Noel? Is Noel a male or female?

2. Describe what the race course is like.

3. What happened between Noel and Cliff the last time they ran this race?

4. Interpret how you think Cliff feels about Noel.

5. Why is it significant that Noel stayed and helped Cliff up after he fell?

6. What evidence is there that it was really an accident? Is Cliff convinced?

7. How does Cliff's experience with Noel compare with an experience that you have had? Explain that experience and how it compares.

8. What solutions would you suggest for Cliff in order to get over his feelings about Noel?

9. What do you think about Noel? What kind of person is he? How can you tell? Evaluate whether or not you could be his friend.

Accident Prone *(cont.)*

Accidents do happen. This is a letter written by Noel. Read the personal letter to help answer the questions at the bottom of the page.

June 16, 2000

Dear Cliff,

   I just wanted to write and let you know how sorry I was about the accident that happened during the race the other day. I never meant to hurt your leg. I truly hope that it is feeling better and that there aren't any scars.

   Coach said that you don't believe me when I say that it was an accident. It was. I didn't even know that I had stepped on you. You didn't say anything in the race to let me know how you felt. You could have said something, don't you think?

   I hope you can forgive me. I want to train with you this summer. You are one of the best runners on the team. Do you think we can make amends?

Sincerely,

Noel

Noel Haversham

---

1. What is the main idea of the letter?

2. How do you think that Cliff feels now that he has read the letter?

3. Do you think that Noel Haversham is sincere? Locate words and phrases that support your opinion.

4. Do you predict that Noel and Cliff will train together in the summer? Why or why not?

Accident Prone *(cont.)*

Document-Based Extension Activities

Work independently or in a small group to complete the following.

1. Look up the meaning of the word *accident*. What does it mean? What is the root of the word? Now look up the word *prone*. What does it mean? Putting the two words together, what does it mean to be accident prone? Would you consider yourself accident prone? Why or why not? Do you know someone who is accident prone? How can you tell when something is an accident?

2. Write your own letter from Noel to Cliff, and then a response letter from Cliff to Noel. What do you think they would say to each other? Print the letter on a letterhead of your choice and compare and contrast your letters with other classmates.

3. Make a list of reasons why the incident between Cliff and Noel was not an accident. Then make a list of reasons why you think it was an accident. Can you find evidence to support either side from the article? Write a persuasive essay trying to convince the reader of the guilt or innocence of Noel. Be sure to support your stance with as much evidence as you can find.

4. Have you had an experience that is similar to the one with Noel and Cliff? What happened? How do you feel about it now? Create a Venn diagram by drawing two circles that interconnect. In the left circle, record the things that make your experience different from the one in the article. In the right circle, record the things that make Cliff and Noel's experience different than yours. Where the circles interconnect, record the things that are similar about the two experiences.

5. There will be many times in your life when you will feel picked on or hurt. Make a poster that lists things a person can do if he or she is hurt or offended by another. Design the poster on the computer and use the graphics and the font changes to emphasize certain points. Hang this poster at your home and school to encourage others to work through these problems and issues.

6. Attend a race in your area. Walk along the course to locate places where an accident like the one described in the article could happen. What is it about a group of people running and racing in a specified area that leads to accidents like this happening? Write an imaginary recommendation to the race officials suggesting ways that they can improve the safety of this course. If you think there are real issues with the safety of this course, then send a copy of this letter to the sponsors or organizers of the race.

The Everglades Forever?

A graceful white bird soars through the sky. In the swamp below, lazy alligators lie still as logs. A tiny frog hops to a lily pad and lets out a big croak. It's just another day in Florida's Everglades. The Everglades is a unique ecosystem found only in the U.S.

The Everglades is about 4,000 square miles of freshwater marsh, rivers, and swamps. Most of the area is covered with grass, which can grow more than six feet high with edges as sharp as saws. The region is home to more than 850 animal species and 900 kinds of plants. Sounds like a natural paradise, right? It used to be. But after years of pollution and other abuse, the Everglades is dying.

Settlers of the Everglades thought the swamp was worthless. They dried out some of the marshy ground. In the 1920s, U.S. government engineers forced the river into a straight path and built canals and dikes to prevent flooding and to keep the water supply stable for new cities. Without its water supply, the Everglades began to shrink. So did its plant and animal populations.

People have drained away too much water and many areas have dried out completely. Animals either leave their homes in search of water or die. At least 56 animal species in the Everglades are threatened or listed as endangered. Large numbers of wading birds, alligators, and sparrows have vanished. Can the Everglades be saved?

Many people refuse to give up without a fight. They want to raise roads, creating overpasses so water can flow under traffic. They want to get rid of some canals, crack down on polluters, and help pass laws to protect the area. One of them, luckily, is Mary Barley. "The Everglades," she says, "is one of our most important natural cathedrals."

Barley is chairwoman of the Everglades Foundation. Her husband, George, started the foundation because he worried about the Everglades' future. Since his death in a 1995 plane crash, Barley and other foundation members have fought on.

Barley has taken on the sugar cane industry. Many sugar growers use fertilizers that contain phosphorous. This chemical runs off into the waters and speeds up the growth of foreign plants. These fast-growing plants use up so much water that native plants die.

Barley knows that even people who want to save the Everglades don't want to pay to correct mistakes others made. She and fellow activists collected 2.5 million signatures. They persuaded Florida voters to pass a state law requiring polluters to pay most of the costs. Thanks to her, a sugar company sold more than 50,000 acres of land back to the state to be restored. The river can run naturally again, which will help bring back native plants and animals.

The Everglades Forever? *(cont.)*

Directions: Answer the questions. You may look at the article.

1. How big is the Everglades?

2. What is the Everglades? Where is it located?

3. Why are people so worried about the Everglades? Why is it significant that Mary Barley calls the Everglades "one of our most important natural cathedrals?"

4. What evidence can you list for reasons to support Mary's cause to save the Everglades?

5. What factors are affecting the life of the Everglades?

6. What solutions would you suggest in order to save the Everglades?

7. Predict what you think would happen if the U.S. government stepped in to help save the Everglades. What would happen to businesses? What would happen to the ecosystem in the Everglades?

8. Do you agree or disagree with Mary Barley and the Everglades Foundation? Explain your answer.

9. Does the author use good evidence in his or her article to save the Everglades? What suggestions would you give to the author?

The Everglades Forever? *(cont.)*

The Everglades National Park is truly a wonder. There are many species and types of animals that call the Everglades home. This is a graph of the number of poisonous and non-poisonous snakes found in the Everglades. Use this graph to answer the questions below.

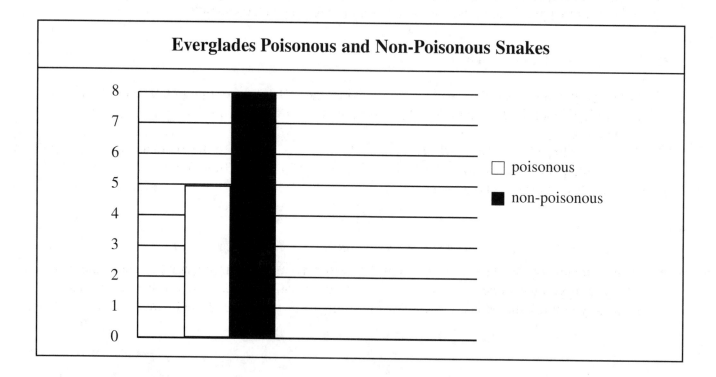

1. There are so many animals that live in the Everglades. What types of animals are being displayed in this graph?

2. Are there more poisonous or non-poisonous snakes found in the everglades? How would the shrinkage of the Everglades affect the number of snakes?

3. If a snake is poisonous, why should we care if it becomes extinct? Explain your answer.

4. How could someone use this graph as justification for saving the Everglades? Explain your answer.

The Everglades Forever? *(cont.)*

Document-Based Extension Activities

Work independently or in a small group to complete the following.

1. Write a statement about the Everglades using the article and the graph as a guide. What can you learn from this graph and article to assist you in making your statement?

2. What can you and your class do to save the Everglades? First, take time to talk about how you as a class feel about the Everglades. What can be done to protect it? Brainstorm a list of ideas. Write out a plan. Who is going to do what? How will you check to see what has been done already? Carry out the plan. Involve others. Educate others. When the plan has been completed, analyze the plan. What worked? What progress has been made? How did the plan work? Was it effective? What should be done next?

3. Write a review of the class project in newsletter format. Post this report on the school Internet Web site, if you have one. Scan pictures of your classmates and their involvement in this cause. How do you think the people involved with saving the Everglades will feel about your efforts?

4. Write an essay on the importance of saving the Everglades and other endangered habitats in the world. What is the problem? What are the issues that prevent these habitats from remaining safe? State your opinion. What evidence can you provide to support your claim?

5. E-mail friends and family informing them about the issue of saving the Everglades and other natural habitats throughout the world. Scan a picture from the Internet or send a link to the Everglades Web page on the Internet. Send a copy of your essay. See what kind of response you will get.

6. Research to learn more about the Everglades. How can you get involved in this issue? What can you do to protect the Everglades? Where can you go to get this information? See if you can make contact with Mary Barley through e-mail or through the postal mail. What suggestions does she have to offer?

On the Prowl Again

On Africa's Serengeti Plain, the mighty roar of a lion is heard for miles around. Wildebeests and zebras raise their ears and run for their lives. They don't want to be a hungry lion's next meal.

For several months, though, a mysterious illness silenced many of the fearsome roars. Between January and September 1994, more than 1,000 lions died in the Serengeti, East Africa's largest wildlife park. It was what one scientist called "the most dramatic die-off of lions anyone has ever seen." No one could explain it.

A team of scientists finally solved the mystery. The lions are feeling better, too. In 1996, a scientific report in *Nature* magazine explained that the lions had died from a disease found mainly in dogs, called canine distemper.

Park rangers first noticed that the lions were behaving strangely. They were twitching madly, did not move about with their usual grace, and hid from the sun. The disease spread quickly among the lions because they constantly lick one another's faces.

"It was very sad," said Heribert Hofer, a German researcher. "You study hundreds of animals and know them as individuals. Suddenly they are dying from something you don't understand."

Scientists studied the body tissues of sick lions and discovered the canine distemper virus. They guessed that the lions caught it from hyenas, which may have picked up the germs at village dumps visited by dogs. Humans living in the area own about 30,000 dogs, and the dog population is growing rapidly.

Scientists are working hard to prevent another outbreak. Giving the lions vaccination shots would be difficult, but researchers are raising money to vaccinate dogs living in the park.

Meanwhile, the lions are rebounding from the deadly virus. Two-thirds of those infected have recovered. The lionesses are eating better. Cubs are surviving longer. Once again, the king of the beasts is announcing his health with that trademark roar.

On the Prowl Again *(cont.)*

Directions: Answer the questions. You may look at the article.

1. What was wrong with the lions? How many lions died between January and September 1994?

2. What do scientists suspect is the mysterious illness that is killing the lions?

3. Summarize how the scientists believe the lions contracted the virus.

4. Describe what scientists are doing to help the lions.

5. What are the benefits of the scientists stepping in to help the lions?

6. Explain the cause and effect of the behaviors and relationship of the lions, the dogs, the hyenas, and the virus.

7. What ideas can you add to the author's ideas to support helping the lions?

8. Do you agree or disagree with helping animals in nature? Explain your answer.

On the Prowl Again *(cont.)*

Lions are fascinating animals. You have just read about the lions in Africa. Lions can also be found in North America. Look at the excerpt from a brochure on lions to answer the questions at the bottom of the page.

The Mighty Mountain Lion

Description

Lions are three to four feet in length. Their long tails can reach three feet long as well. Mountain lions weigh between 70 to 170 pounds.

The mountain lion is a large, slender cat with a small head and a very long tail.

Lions are light brown and sometimes can appear gray or almost black, depending on how the lighting is.

Mountain lions can also be known as a cougar, puma, panther, painter, and a catamount.

Eating and Living

Lions are known to be secretive animals. They live alone except during breeding time.

Mountain lions are meat-eaters. Some of their favorite meals include deer, rabbit, rodents, and jackrabbits. Lions have also been known to eat livestock or dogs.

Habitat and Distribution

The mountain lion can be found in many places and is more spread out than any other wild cat. Mountain lions can be found from Canada to South America.

Mountain lions are found mostly in remote secluded areas of the southwestern United States, as well as western Canada and much of Mexico.

There is a small number of lions still found in southern Florida, but this species is considered to be endangered.

The mountain lion can also be found in Texas. Here it is not endangered and is considered a healthy species. Mountain lions are classified as unprotected. Though they are not protected, mountain lions can be found in more countries than they were ten years ago.

1. What is the purpose of this brochure? What type of information can you learn from this brochure?

2. How do the lions in North America compare to the lions found in Africa?

3. Scientists were concerned about the deadly virus attacking lions in Africa. Based on the living and eating habits of the lions in North America, do you think they run the risk of catching the same type of deadly virus?

4. Describe the impact that cities and towns can have on wildlife.

On the Prowl Again *(cont.)*

Document-Based Extension Activities

Work independently or in a small group to complete the following.

1. Based on the brochure and the information in the article, do you think changes are necessary to save lions in the future? When do you think people should get involved in the protection of wild animals? When does the protection of wildlife go too far?

2. What criteria could be used to determine when people should step in to save wildlife? What are the pros and cons of intervening on behalf of wildlife, whether it be plants or animals?

3. What laws have been passed in your area concerning the protection of wildlife? How do these laws compare or contrast with those in Africa? How can you find out?

4. Write an essay expressing your opinion of the lions in Africa and the canine distemper disease.

5. Design a poster that scientists could post to try and save the lions.

6. Write a journal entry as if you were a scientist trying to save the lions. What would it feel like to watch these lions die and not know why? How would you feel about the lions?

7. Research the lions of Africa. What do they eat? What do they need to survive? Why are they threatened? What is their habitat like? Has there been a lion bred in captivity? Analyze your findings. What suggestions can you make to the scientists about what to do to protect the lions?

Shipwrecked in Antarctica

When Ernest Shackleton packed for his trip to Antarctica in July of 1914, he seemed ready for anything. Among the items stowed in his ship were cans of meat, a miniature pool table, a banjo, lanterns, a bicycle, and soccer balls. Shackleton hoped to become the first person to travel across the frozen continent at the bottom of the world. Nothing could have prepared Shackleton or his crew for what did happen, though. Instead of crossing Antarctica, they made history in one of the most incredible survival stories ever.

Breathtaking photos of the doomed trip have been published for the first time in two books: for kids, Jennifer Armstrong's *Shipwreck at the Bottom of the World* (Crown); for adults, Caroline Alexander's *The Endurance* (Knopf). The pictures were taken by a photographer, Frank Hurler, who, along with 26 sailors and scientists and 69 sled dogs, went with Shackleton on the expedition.

Shackleton's last stop before heading for Antarctica was a whaling station on South Georgia Island. Norwegian whalers told the crew that it was "a bad year for ice."

They were right. Upon entering the Weddell Sea, Shackleton was forced to zigzag through dangerous ice sheets, sometimes passing 400 icebergs a day! On January 18, 1915, the ice closed around the ship.

Although he was less than 100 miles from Antarctica, Shackleton soon realized he could not possibly cross the continent that winter. The crew would have to wait.

The ship was locked in ice for nearly ten months. By October 1915, the ice was crushing its thick wooden walls. Shackleton ordered the crew to leave. They grabbed what they could, including 150 of Hurler's precious photos.

The sailors struggled to reach land on three lifeboats they dragged across ice and rowed through frigid waters. Eventually, they reached Elephant Island, but it was deserted. So Shackleton bravely set out again with five of his strongest men. They sailed and rowed 800 miles in a tiny boat, battling high waves, winds, and severe thirst. Finally, they landed at South Georgia Island.

Four months after Shackleton sailed away, one of the men on Elephant Island spotted a ship offshore. When it came closer, the crew recognized Shackleton. They were rescued! All 28 members of the *Endurance* reached home safely. Shackleton was a true hero.

Shipwrecked in Antarctica *(cont.)*

Directions: Answer the questions. You may look at the article.

1. Who was Ernest Shackleton and what was he planning to do in July of 1914?

2. Shackleton and his crew prepared to make history, but how did their story change?

3. Describe what it must have been like to live in a ship that was locked in ice for nearly ten months.

4. Explain why Shackleton ordered the crew to leave the ship in October of 1915.

5. Shackleton was a hero because he bravely faced the frigid waters to get help. Can you think of a time in your life when you had to be brave and strong to make it through? Explain your answer.

6. Compare and contrast Shackleton and Christopher Columbus. How are their experiences the same? How are they different?

7. What do you predict the response of the stranded men on Elephant Island was when they saw Shackleton had returned for them?

8. What is the message of this article? Do you think that the message was accurately portrayed?

Shipwrecked in Antarctica *(cont.)*

Antarctica has always been a place to explore. There are so many things to discover about this continent. Scientists have been researching Antarctica and it's climate, wildlife, and environment for many years. Exploring Antarctica has its dangers, though. Look at the map below detailing the experiences of Shackleton to answer the questions.

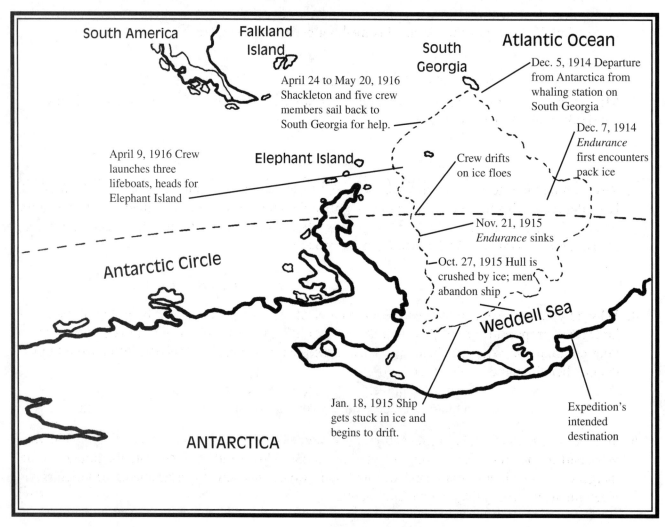

1. How many days was the *Endurance* forcing its way through ice?

2. What does the map portray? What bodies of water did the *Endurance* sail through?

3. Write a journal entry from the Shackleton's journal describing his experience. What do you think Shackleton learned?

Shipwrecked in Antarctica *(cont.)*

Document-Based Extension Activities

Work independently or in a small group to complete the following.

1. Look at the map that shows the route that Shackleton and his crew took on their voyage to Antarctica. Create a new time line that shows these steps. What types of events might have been on the time line had Shackleton and his men not been successful?

2. Make a list of contributions that Shackleton's group made for other explorers. Why is it easy to overlook some of these contributions?

3. Research on the Internet, or with other sources, the experiences of other explorers of Antarctica. How did these trips turn out? Were they successful? How have these trips made a difference for others? Have a group discussion on the process these explorers went through to accomplish their goals. Discuss what can be learned from the process.

4. Why do you think someone related to the men of Shackleton's crew would be proud of them? Draw up a proposal for a display of explorers that have made a difference in the early days of your community. What can be done to honor these early settlers or pioneers? How would this display benefit and educate others?

5. Write a fictional newspaper article about the experience of Shackleton's crew. Imagine that you were part of the crew. How would you tell the story? How would you educate the public on the dangers involved in a mission such as this? Why would this newspaper article be beneficial? Keep the news article informative and motivating.

6. Interview a person at a museum and find out what it takes to get approval for the museum, the gathering of artifacts, the security of the items displayed, and security necessary for museums. How can this information help you with your community display?

7. Brainstorm a list of items that you think are needed to go on a trip to Antarctica. Think of a new invention that could be used. Draw up a design of what your invention would look like. How could this invention have helped Shackleton and his crew? If time and materials are available, make a prototype of your design.

Dinosaurs with Feathers

In the summer of 1996, a farmer in northeast China was digging in a dried-up lake. He dug up some strange-looking fossilized bones. He wondered: "Could these be the remains of an ancient dragon?"

Not quite. The bones actually belonged to an ancient meat-eating dinosaur called Sinosauropteryx prima (*sine-o-sore-opp-terr-oiks pree-ma*). The creature, which was close to the size of a large chicken, lived about 120 million years ago.

Size may not have been the only thing this dinosaur had in common with the chicken. Scientists made a surprising announcement—Sinosauropteryx might have had tiny feathers!

That's not as crazy as it may sound. Most experts think today's pigeons and parrots are related to dinosaurs. Some even argue that birds are dinosaurs, the one branch of the dinosaur family tree that has survived.

Many scientists had wondered whether some dinosaurs had feathers. But feathers are so fragile that they usually rot away without a trace. Luckily, the Sinosauropteryx fossils showed a lot of detail. "I had been skeptical of the claim that the dinosaur had feathers," says Canadian scientist Phil Currie. "Boy, was I impressed!"

Not everyone is convinced. Some bird experts suggest that the feather-like structures may be bits and pieces of scales. Whatever they are, they are not the right size and shape for flying. They may have been used to keep the dinosaur warm or help it attract a mate.

When and why feathers first appeared on the earth is just one puzzle scientists hope to solve by studying the area where the fossils were found. "These beds date to a time when modern mammals, flowering plants, and birds first appeared," says Alan Brush, a bird expert at the University of Connecticut. "The discovery of this site is just as important as going to Mars."

Dinosaurs with Feathers *(cont.)*

Directions: Answer the questions. You may look at the article.

1. What animals do some scientists think dinosaurs are related to?

2. What did the Chinese farmer discover in 1996? Why are these findings significant?

3. Summarize how feathers would be helpful to a dinosaur, if they couldn't help a dinosaur fly?

4. Explain what some scientists have said to discount the theory of dinosaurs having feathers.

5. Compare the pros and cons of having two different viewpoints. How can two different viewpoints be helpful in learning about the dinosaurs of so long ago?

6. What kind of evidence is needed to prove the theory that some dinosaurs had feathers?

7. What is the author's opinion of whether or not dinosaurs had feathers? What evidence in the article supports your answer?

8. What criteria would you use to assess the validity of research findings? How would you go about determining whether or not something was relevant?

Dinosaurs with Feathers *(cont.)*

Scientists have found evidence that make them wonder whether or not some dinosaurs had feathers. They are trying to find more evidence to support this theory. Do you think that it is possible that dinosaurs had feathers? We know many birds that have feathers today. Use the Venn diagram comparing the dinosaur and the chicken to answer the questions below.

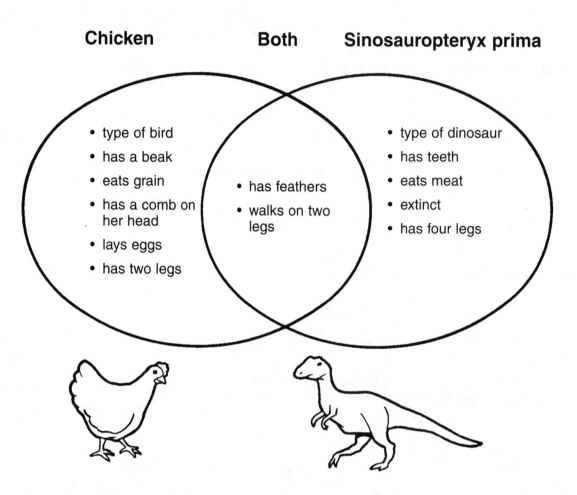

Chicken   **Both**   **Sinosauropteryx prima**

- type of bird
- has a beak
- eats grain
- has a comb on her head
- lays eggs
- has two legs

- has feathers
- walks on two legs

- type of dinosaur
- has teeth
- eats meat
- extinct
- has four legs

1. What does the Venn diagram compare? Are there more similarities or differences between the dinosaur and the chicken?

2. What do you think scientists can learn about dinosaurs by studying chickens and other animals with feathers?

3. How would dinosaurs use feathers? How do chickens use their feathers?

4. How can scientists convince the general public that some dinosaurs had feathers?

Dinosaurs with Feathers *(cont.)*

Document-Based Extension Activities

Work independently or in a small group to complete the following.

1. Analyze the information you have learned from the article and from the graphic. Design a plan to address how to prove whether or not dinosaurs had feathers. List the reasons you can find for supporting this claim. List the reasons for not supporting this claim. Which viewpoint do you believe? What are the tradeoffs for your decision?

2. Write a persuasive essay convincing the reader to either support the fact that dinosaurs had feathers or NOT to support the fact that dinosaurs had feathers. Remember you need to have plenty of evidence to support your opinion. You also need to be very clear on what your opinion is. Here are some questions to consider as you write your essay:

   • What is your viewpoint on dinosaurs and feathers?
   • What is your view on how well the scientists have made their argument?
   • Are there options to these two opinions on dinosaurs?
   • How are you going to convince the reader?
   • Who is your audience? How can you appeal to the audience?
   • What evidence can you use to support your opinion?

3. Research to find more evidence about the dinosaurs mentioned in the article. What do other articles and references claim? Do they add more or less support to your theory?

4. Compare and contrast how different groups of scientists research and form their theories. Are there similarities? What are the differences?

5. Have a debate with other members of your class on whether or not dinosaurs had feathers. Have both sides represented in the debate. Gather sufficient evidence to put together a compelling argument. Practice your debate skills. Anticipate your opponent's points and be prepared. Practice with a partner before you begin.

How Vikings Lived

Greenland is not very green at all. In fact, most of the world's largest island is frozen. It is buried beneath a lot of snow.

More than a thousand years ago, Erik the Red, a Viking explorer, left his home in Iceland. He had discovered a rich supply of fish, whales, walruses, and seals in Greenland's waters. He needed help to get the riches, however. He guessed that an attractive name might get fellow Vikings from their cold homeland to an even colder place. So he called the new land Greenland.

Some Vikings must have been tricked by the name. About 5,000 Vikings packed up long ships and made the dangerous trip. They began exploring. Families set up homes called fjords (fee-yords).

Scientists thought they had found all of the Viking settlements. In 1992, however, Inuit hunters stumbled across some unusual pieces of wood floating into a fjord near the capital city. They had found a lost Viking settlement.

Now a team of scientists from around the world has finished the job of exploring it. Known as the "village beneath the sand," the settlement was actually a large farm where Vikings lived for more than 300 years. Six buildings of stone and peat (rotted moss and other plants) had up to 30 rooms each.

Digging through ancient storerooms and kitchens, the scientists found a treasure chest of Viking daily life. They found kitchen utensils, walrus-tooth dice, and reindeer-bone necklaces. Miniature boats and wooden boxes may have been children's toys. "It was a hard life," the scientists say, "but not without its comforts."

How Vikings Lived (cont.)

Directions: Answer the questions. You may look at the article.

1. What is the world's largest island?

2. What is a fjord?

3. Summarize why Erik the Red was trying to lure other Vikings to come to Greenland. Why did he choose the name Greenland?

4. Describe what a typical day in the life of a family in Greenland during this time period would have been like.

5. What evidence do the scientists have that a Viking settlement was indeed found in 1992?

6. Why do you think the Vikings left Greenland?

7. What if the Vikings had stayed? What would life be like in Greenland today?

8. Assess how well you think scientists are able to determine what life was like in the past based on artifacts and other remnants found. Can we trust their theories and assumptions?

9. Do you agree with the facts presented in the article? Did the author state a main idea and then support it with evidence?

How Vikings Lived (cont.)

Look at the pictures related to Vikings. What can be learned from these pictures about the Vikings' way of life? Use the pictures below to answer the questions at the bottom of the page.

1. What do you think is the purpose for the helmet and the shield that the Viking in the picture wears? Why do you think the Vikings needed armor?

2. What type of personal qualities would one have to possess in order to be a Viking?

3. Based on the pictures, what do you think the temperature and climate of the land where the Vikings lived was like? Explain your answer.

4. Compare and contrast your life with that of a Viking. How is your life similar? Different?

How Vikings Lived *(cont.)*

Document-Based Extension Activities

Work independently or in a small group to complete the following.

1. Write a message about the pictures of the Vikings on the previous page. What does your message say? Exchange with another student in the class and read each other's messages. Did you both learn similar things from these pictures of Vikings?

2. What is difficult about using an artist's rendition of how things looked as opposed to seeing actual photographs? How might this transfer to the gathering of research from ancient civilizations?

3. Analyze each picture. What is it about that picture that helps you understand the Vikings better? Make a list of assumptions about the Vikings. How did they sleep? What did they eat? How did they play? Where did they live?

4. What can you learn about the culture of the Vikings by analyzing the pictures? Make a comparison between what you know about the community Vikings lived in and the city that you live in. How are things different? How are they similar?

5. Finish the following sentence: *The Vikings remind me of. . .* Think of something in your life that you are reminded of when you hear or think about the Vikings. Is there something from their civilization that you can relate to?

6. The Vikings lived many years ago. Write an essay about the way your life is structured in comparison to the Viking's way of life. You will need to gather research and information.

7. Write a news article about the events in Greenland during the reign of the Vikings. Answer the questions: who, what, where, when, why, and how. Write the article as if it would be printed in today's newspaper. Type the news article into the computer and select a graphic/photo to accompany your story.

Open Wide, Don't Bite!

Dentist Peter Kertesz of London has the wildest patients in the world. On Fridays, after a week of treating people, this dentist treats animals with very large teeth.

Kertesz treats animals ranging from aardvarks to zebras. It all started when a veterinarian asked the dentist to pull teeth from a cat. "Never again," he thought.

But soon he was taking on bigger cats – lions, tigers, and jaguars – and then elephants (which have molars the size of bricks), camels, bears, monkeys, wolves, and even whales. He has treated about 50 types of animals in all.

Recently he removed a tusk from a five-ton zoo elephant in Germany. He used a four-inch drill bit. Drugs keep the animals quiet and pain-free while Kertesz works. He works along with a team of vets and assistants.

Large animals, such as lions, are easiest to work with. This is because there is so much room in their mouths. The toughest patients are aardvarks. Their mouths open only about an inch.

Kertesz has taken his dental skills to eight countries. Most of his work is for zoos. Circuses and veterinary hospitals also call him. He has worked on Siberian tigers in Russia. He has worked on an elephant in Spain. He has even worked on a gorilla, a jaguar, badgers, deer, and foxes in England.

A bad tooth can keep an animal from hunting, eating, and even mating. The dental work helps animals live longer. They can also live healthier lives. "The mouth is the gateway to the existence of all animals," he says.

Open Wide, Don't Bite! *(cont.)*

Directions: Answer the questions. You may look at the article.

1. What does dentist Peter Kertesz of London do after working with human teeth all week?

2. How many species of animals has he treated?

3. How did Kertesz begin his work with animals? What was his first reaction? Why do you think he continued?

4. Summarize how Kertesz feels about helping animals and humans have good dental health.

5. Make a list of the things you would have to remember when working with animals and their teeth.

6. Compare and contrast treating the dental needs of humans and animals? How are they alike? How are they different?

7. Animals obviously don't use a toothbrush to clean their teeth. How do you think animals clean their teeth?

8. The author uses comparisons in the article to help the reader understand what it would be like to work with these animals and their teeth. Evaluate how you think the comparisons help get the message across to the reader.

9. The author ends the article with a quote by Kertesz. Why is this an effective ending?

Open Wide, Don't Bite! *(cont.)*

Dentist Peter Kertesz works on both human and animal teeth. What must it be like to work on these different sets of teeth. Use the picture of the lion teeth on the left, and the picture of a set of human teeth on the right, to answer the questions at the bottom of the page.

Lion Teeth   **Human Teeth**

1. What is the difference between the lion's teeth and the human teeth?

2. What would be the pros and cons of working on animal teeth as opposed to human teeth?

3. Humans deal with cavities, gingivitis, and other teeth and mouth diseases. Looking at the lion's teeth, do you think lions have to worry about the same things humans do?

4. How would the diet of a lion promote or demote good dental health?

Open Wide, Don't Bite! (cont.)

Document-Based Extension Activities

Work independently or in a small group to complete the following.

1. How has the dentist in this article made a difference to the animals he has helped? How does this dentist inform others about taking care of animals? Make a list of the achievements that this dentist has made to the practice of dentistry and the issue of caring for animals. Are there other dentists who have played a significant role in the lives of others? Who are they and what contributions have they made?

2. Look back at the article. How did this dentist get involved with working on animal teeth in the beginning? Is he certain this is what he wants to do? What do you think caused the dentist to reevaluate his decision?

3. Create a survey you can use to poll students in your school. Be sure to survey a large number of students to get an accurate view. Here are some questions to consider:

   - Do you think that dentists should work on animals? Animals have no way of telling you how something feels.
   - Do you think a dentist of animals should have special training? Treating animal teeth can't be the same as treating human teeth.
   - What are the pros and cons of working with animals?
   - How do you think animals feel about people working on their teeth?
   - What is the reason for working on animal teeth in the first place?
   - What contributions do people like this dentist make in our society?

4. Look back at your poll. Were you surprised by your findings, or did you get the answers you were expecting? What is the general consensus of how the students in your school think about animals receiving dental care?

5. Write a newspaper article about the dentist, Peter Kertesz. What do you think other dentists will think? Make a prediction on what Kertesz will do long after his days of working on human teeth are over?

6. What advice do you have for the dentist? Write a letter to Peter Kertesz with your recommendations. What should he do and why? Try to incorporate the information you received from polling other students. How do you think Peter Kertesz will feel about your letter?

A Special Delivery

Something was definitely up in the platypus pen. Koorina, a female, and "N," a male, were spending quite a bit of time together. They live in a sanctuary in Melbourne, Australia. Then, on November 14, 1998, Koorina was seen gathering bunches of leaves. She tucked them under her paddle-like tail. She lugged them to a spot she had hollowed out under the roots of a tree. For five days she disappeared inside her burrow.

The platypus experts, Holland and Fisk, could hardly contain their excitement. Could it be that Koorina was busy laying eggs? If so, she was only the second captive platypus ever to do so.

Over the next few weeks, a video camera filmed what the platypus did. This allowed Fisk and Holland to observe the shy, duck-billed mammal without disturbing her. They watched in awe as Koorina ate huge quantities of worms, bugs, and crayfish. She was preparing to nurse her young. Soon she was eating one and a half times her weight in food a day!

In early December, Koorina made platypus history. Deep inside her burrow, two leathery grape-size eggs hatched. The tiny newborns each weighed less than a nickel. They had long lips that would later become beaks.

The world did not get a look at the babies for six months. On April 3, 1999, they left the safety of their burrow. Fisk, who has spent ten years trying to breed captive platypuses, said this was "the biggest and best thing in my life!"

The last time a platypus was born in captivity was during World War II. Corrie, born in 1944, made the front-page news around the world. Though later attempts to breed the mammals failed, Fisk believed he could do it. He said the animals were "comfortable with their burrow and the weather conditions were perfect." Perhaps most important of all, platypus love had bloomed. "Basically, 'N' and Koorina like each other."

One of the babies was put on display at the sanctuary in April 1999.

A Special Delivery *(cont.)*

Directions: Answer the questions. You may look at the article.

1. Who are Koorina and "N"? Where do they live?

2. How long did it take before the world got a good look at the babies?

3. Explain what is so amazing about the delivery of the platypus babies.

4. Give examples from the article that show how amazing this accomplishment is.

5. What did the conditions need to be like for the platypus to be born in captivity?

6. Explain why attempts to breed egg-laying mammals in captivity have failed.

7. What if the babies had not survived? Would history still have been made? How would this change the story?

8. Summarize the characteristics of Fisk's personality that make him successful.

9. Write a recommendation of what another scientist should do in order to attempt breeding a platypus in captivity. What advice would you suggest?

A Special Delivery *(cont.)*

The platypus is an amazing animal. Use the following picture to answer the questions at the bottom of the page.

1. Looking at the picture above, what kind of habitat does a platypus need in order to survive?

2. What type of food do you think a platypus would eat?

3. Why do you think it is rare to have a platypus reproduce in captivity?

4. What challenges would you encounter if you were to set up a platypus habitat?

A Special Delivery (cont.)

Document-Based Extension Activities

Work independently or in a small group to complete the following.

1. Research the platypus. What kind of animal is this? What characteristics are unique to the platypus? Write a research report on your findings. Be sure to visit the school or public library to get as much information as you can. Draw a picture of a platypus to accompany your report.

2. Write a newspaper article about the birth of the platypus babies in captivity. In writing your article, be sure to answer the questions who, what, where, when, why, and how. Think of a creative introduction for your newspaper article and be sure to have a "catchy" headline. Type your article into the computer using a newspaper format.

3. Create a brochure on the platypus. Using the computer, include graphics, headings, typeface, diagrams and more. Make this informational brochure stand out. If possible, print it on a color printer to give it color. Use this brochure as a means to share what you have learned about the platypus.

4. Write an adventure story about Koorina and "N." Start at the beginning with their birth in captivity. What happened next? What will be the next adventure? Be sure that your story is factual and accurate. This should be a fictional story that is based on true facts. This is a creative way to share your new knowledge on the platypus.

5. Create a "help wanted" poster for Fisk, the person in the article who worked to breed the platypus babies. What type of characteristics does a person like this need to have to be successful? What skills does this person need to have? Advertise for a person like this on your poster. Design your poster and print it on the computer. Be sure to enlarge the font and pictures so it can be seen from a distance.

6. Interview a zookeeper in your area. Brainstorm beforehand a list of questions that you can ask so that you are prepared for the interview. Some questions might include:

   - What does it take to care for an animal in captivity?
   - Have you heard about the platypus babies born to Koorina and "N"? What do you think?
   - Why is it more difficult to breed an animal in captivity than in the wild?
   - In your opinion, are there some animals that should never be held captive?
   - Do you have any experiences with breeding wild animals?
   - What do you like about your job? How does somebody get a job like yours?

Troubled Tongues

Leroy Sealy's first day of first grade was probably the loneliest day of his life. He couldn't speak to any of the kids in his class and he couldn't understand a thing they were saying. "I was pretty much alone because I couldn't communicate," says Sealy, a Choctaw Native American. "I didn't learn English until starting school." Sealy knew only the Choctaw language, and no one in his class could speak it.

Sealy is now 33, and a professor of Choctaw at the University of Oklahoma in Norman. He still speaks Choctaw, as do about 12,000 people, but he is worried about the future of his native language. Choctaw is on the endangered-language list.

When you hear the words *endangered* or *extinct*, you may think of rhinos, tigers, and other wildlife. But languages can also become endangered and extinct. People say about half the world's 6,500 languages are in trouble. Some have fewer than five living speakers, and nearly 3,000 may disappear in the next 100 years.

Linguists, people who study languages, are working to save endangered languages. One group doing this work is the Endangered Language Fund. They just awarded *$10,000* for ten language-preservation projects. The money will be used to make recordings of languages so the words won't be lost forever.

How does a language become endangered? "The most common cause is that a small community comes into close contact with a larger one, and people begin using the dominant language," says linguist Doug Whalen. Better technology and transportation have spread more common languages, including English, across the planet. Native languages are used less.

Sealy says governments have also hurt native languages. "Native American children sent to government schools in the 1950s and 1960s were told not to speak their native languages either, believing that English would help them economically in life. This caused many languages to be lost."

Why should we care? "Every language has its way of expressing ideas about the world," explains Whalen. "When a language dies, we lose that insight."

Many endangered tongues face another threat—young people who have no interest in speaking the language of their ancestors. Sealy hopes young Native Americans will learn to value their cultural heritage and language.

"My niece is in fourth grade. She is learning Choctaw, and although she mostly speaks English, she understands Choctaw when we speak with her," says Sealy. "We encourage her because the younger generations will be the ones to carry the language into the 21st century."

Troubled Tongues (cont.)

Directions: Answer the questions. You may look at the article.

1. What is Choctaw?

2. What is an endangered language? How does a language become endangered?

3. Summarize in your own words why Leroy Sealy is concerned about the Choctaw language becoming extinct.

4. Why is it significant that the Endangered Language Fund is giving money to preserve endangered languages?

5. How does Patricia Sealy, the fourth grader, feel about learning Choctaw? Explain your answer.

6. Predict what will happen to the language of the Choctaw Native Americans. Why do you think so? Explain your answer.

7. Why would the government not want people to speak their native languages?

8. Using today's technology, how would you suggest that some of these endangered languages be saved?

9. Assess how you think this article can help protect and save languages. What is the purpose of this article?

Troubled Tongues (cont.)

The Choctaw language is on the verge of extinction. The Choctaw language can be translated into English. Use the chart of the Choctaw and English languages to answer the questions at the bottom of the page.

Common Phrases in Choctaw Translated	
Choctaw	**English**
Halito	Hello
Chim achukma?	Are you well?
A, chishnato?	Yes, and you?
A, vm achukmah akinlih.	Yes, I am well, too.
ikana	friend
Chi hohchifo nanta?	What is your name?
Sa hohchifo ut . . .	My name is . . . .
Achukma hoke	It is good, (or) I am fine.
onahinli achukma	Good morning.
Yakoke	Thank you.
Ant chukoa	Come in.
Kucha	Go out!
Minti	Come here!
chi pisala hakinli	I'll see you later.
Binili (Bininili)	Sit down.
Hikia	Stand up.
Sa yoshoba	I am lost.
Ak akostinincho	I don't understand.
Akostininchi li	I understand.
Salaha hosh anumpoli	Please speak slowly.

1. What two languages are shown in the chart?

2. Using the chart, how would you say, "Hello, are you well? Please speak slowly," in the Choctaw language?

3. Compare and contrast the English and Choctaw languages.

4. The Choctaw Native Americans are concerned that their language will become extinct. Looking at these words from the Choctaw language, what would make it hard to preserve this language?

Troubled Tongues *(cont.)*

Document-Based Extension Activities

Work independently or in a small group to complete the following.

1. Read through the phrases again of the Choctaw language. What does this chart say about the Choctaw Native Americans? Make a list of observations you can make about the Choctaw based on their language.

2. How many times have you tried to learn a new language? Write a journal entry as though you are a young person trying to learn Choctaw. How would you feel? How would things be different than speaking your own language?

3. How does learning a new language make a difference in your life? Make a list of positive things that happen in your life as a result of learning a new language. Don't forget to include things like making new friends, learning about a different culture, stretching your knowledge, experiencing new things, etc.

4. Write a newspaper article about the problem of some languages becoming extinct. Research on the Internet and use the article you just read as a reference. Using statistics and facts can help support your claim.

5. Interview a person who is knowledgeable about the Choctaw language or another endangered language. Some questions you might consider asking include the following:

   - What is the language and how long has it been around?
   - Why is this language becoming extinct or endangered?
   - How much money does it cost to keep this language in existence?
   - How many people still speak this language?
   - Are there any young people interested in learning this language?
   - What can people do to prevent languages from becoming extinct?

6. Brainstorm a list of things that can be done to keep this language alive and well. What can be done to educate others as to the value of teaching their children their native language? Do you take advantage of the opportunities to learn a new language?

7. Interview a grandparent or an older neighbor. Ask them about languages they know. Have they shared this knowledge with the next generation? How can this language and this culture be passed on from generation to generation?

A Sweet Deal

Bridget Hickson, 13, starts each school day with a pop—the sugary, fizzy kind. The seventh-grader in New York City drinks one 20-ounce bottle of Coke or Sprite before classes begin at 8 A.M. At lunchtime, she guzzles two more bottles of soda pop. "I like the way it tickles my throat," she says. Total cost for the three bottles of bubbly pop: $2.70. Total teaspoonfuls of sugar in the three bottles: about 50.

Bridget's passion for pop is not that unusual. Kids today are drinking more soda than ever before, and many are buying it in school. In 1997, kids spent $750 million on soda, candy, and chips in school vending machines!

While soda companies get much of that money, schools keep some, too. Money from soda machine sales helps pay for books, computers, sports programs, and after-school activities. School officials say they cannot afford to lose those funds.

But health experts are concerned that selling sugary soda in schools encourages poor nutrition. They point out that a 12-ounce can of soda contains ten teaspoonfuls of sugar and has no vitamins or protein. They want schools to unplug their soda machines.

In Florida, the school soda machine debate has recently exploded like a shaken-up can of you-know-what. In March 1999, Florida's Governor Jeb Bush asked the Department of Education to make it easier for high school kids to buy soft drinks. Bush supports soda sales because they sweeten school budgets.

Since 1997, students in Florida have not been allowed to use school soft-drink machines until one hour after lunch. The rule is intended to encourage kids to buy milk and other healthy drinks at lunchtime. But as a result, schools in Florida are collecting fewer dollars from soda sales. John Fox, the athletic director in Duvall County, Florida, says sports programs in his county have lost $450,000 since the vending-machine restrictions began two years ago. That money was supposed to fund "everything from transportation to new uniforms," says Fox. For now, new uniforms will have to wait.

"Soda pop is junk," declares nutritionist Michael Jacobson. "It has no vitamins, no minerals, no protein, and no fiber." Jacobson is the director of the Center for Science in the Public Interest and the author of "Liquid Candy," a 1998 report on the health effects of soft drinks. Heaping helpings of sugar from soft drinks can lead to many health problems, including obesity and tooth decay.

In addition, kids who fill up on soda instead of more nutritious foods miss out on important vitamins and minerals. Choosing soda over milk, for example, prevents some kids from getting the calcium they need to build strong bones and teeth.

What do you think? Are soda machines in schools a good idea or too much of a threat to kids' health?

A Sweet Deal (cont.)

Directions: Answer the questions. You may look at the article.

1. Why is soda considered junk?

2. How much money did school kids spend on soda, candy, and chips in school vending machines in 1997?

3. What is the problem with drinking soda instead of milk?

4. Which state is mentioned specifically in support of the soda vending machines in schools? Why is the governor of this state in support of selling soda at schools?

5. Make a list comparing the pros and cons of selling soda in school.

6. Is soda sold at your school? What do you think about it? Are soda machines in schools a good idea or too much of a threat to kids' health?

7. What if schools were able to receive funding from other sources instead of the vending machines? How would this change the debate of whether or not soda should be available at school?

8. Compose a fictional letter to the local school board supporting or opposing the idea of vending machines in your school. Be sure to support your opinion with facts and information presented in the article.

9. Can you tell how the author feels about the soda machines in school? Locate examples from the text to support your opinion.

A Sweet Deal *(cont.)*

Soda consumption has risen in the last twenty years. What does this mean? The graph below shows the amount of soda and milk consumed by boys and girls. It compares the amount of soda consumption at different times in history.

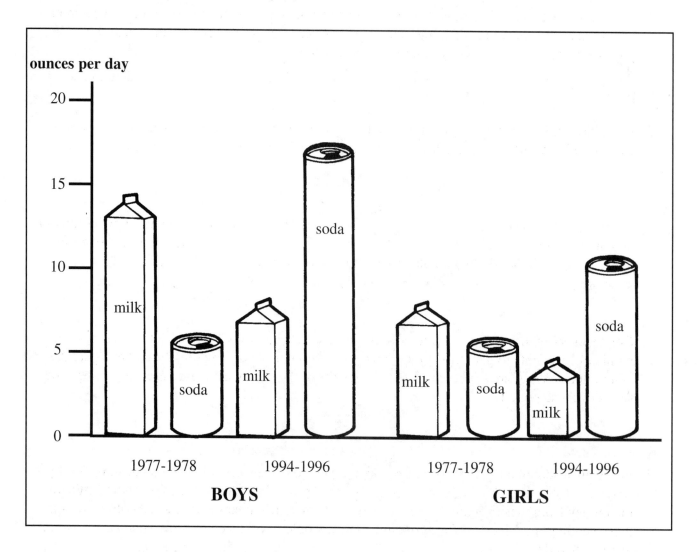

1. How many ounces of milk did boys drink between 1977-1978?

2. According to the graph, do boys or girls drink more soda? Why do you think this is so?

3. Kids are drinking less and less milk. Why do you think this is so?

4. Kids drink more soda than milk these days. How will this have an effect on kids? Explain your answer.

A Sweet Deal *(cont.)*

Document-Based Extension Activities

Work independently or in a small group to complete the following.

1. Brainstorm with a small group of students what information you need to determine your opinion about whether kids are drinking too much soda. Make a list of things you know and things that you still need to know before you make your decision.

2. Look back at the article and the graph. What type of research was done to support the opinion expressed in the article? Make a list of these items and use them in your research.

3. Research soda consumption across the United States. Has it gone up or down? Why? Find out how many children drink soda on a daily basis in your school. If possible, interview some of these children. What do they think about the issue of drinking so much soda?

4. Create a survey that you can use to poll the students in your school. Be sure to survey a large number of students to get an accurate view. Use the same survey to poll the teachers, parents, and other adults. What are the results? Are the results of the survey different based on the age and status of those polled?

5. Interview a school administrator to find out the position of the school on soda consumption by students. Does the school administration support the vending machines in the school? Where is the money from these vending machines spent? How much money does the school make from these vending machines? What programs, if any, would have to be cut if the vending machines were removed?

6. Attend a school council or a staff meeting. Take notes about how changes are made and accepted. See if you can get a copy of the school district's policy on vending machines.

7. Analyze your findings. Write an essay on whether or not you think the students should have access to soda on the school campus. Be sure to cite your evidence and research to support your ideas.

Ratings War

Annie Suzak's mom and dad now have an answer to the question they love to ask when Annie watches TV. Annie, 13, of Oak Park, Illinois, says, "My parents always ask, 'Is that show for kids?' With the ratings, they can make sure I'm not lying."

In January 1997, network TV got a new ratings system to keep kids honest and parents informed. Shows on ABC, NBC, CBS, Fox and other channels are now tagged with coded ratings intended to help parents decide what kids should watch. In addition, all new TVs, 13 inches or larger, will contain a V-chip. The V-chip will allow parents to screen out any shows they do not want their kids to watch. Ratings and V-chips are great ways to make sure television is a good influence on kids.

The codes appear in the upper-left-hand corner of the TV screen for the first 15 seconds of a 30-minute show. They are similar to movie ratings. The ratings system tells what audience a show is suited for: G (everyone), PG (parental guidance suggested), TV-14 (kids 14 and older), or TV-M (mature audiences). Some networks also use a code telling parents why they may object to a particular show. For instance, a show may be rated TV-14 because of nasty words, violence, or racy love scenes, or perhaps all three. The code would then read L (for language), V (for violence), and S (for sex). "Tell parents what's in the show, and let them decide what is appropriate for their kids," says Vicky Rideout of Children Now in Oakland, California.

The ratings era started with a new law passed in February 1996. By January 1, 2000, according to the law, all new TVs must be made with the V-chip. This tiny computer chip lets parents block out shows with certain ratings.

The government and TV industry people who created the new system wisely left room for changes. "We might be able to make it better," President Clinton said. "The advocacy groups deserve to be heard and considered. But we are now doing what I think ought to be done."

The new system is good because it helps kids and parents discuss kids' TV choices. Many families already have ways of choosing TV shows; the new system will not change their viewing habits. Colin Wilson, a ninth-grader in Fort Worth, Texas, says they won't change what he watches. He often gets to pick his own shows. "I trust his judgement," says his mom, Claudia Wilson. "The ratings system may be helpful to some people, but basic common sense works equally well." The system will especially help people with younger children, however.

Stephen Barnes, 12, of Brooklyn, New York, thinks a TV-M rating might tempt kids who are flipping channels. But what kids see in movies and video games is often more violent or grown-up than TV shows, he says. "Most parents don't know what their kids watch, anyway."

One of the best features of the new system is that it depends on the involvement of parents. Some parents have already laid down the rules. "I'm allowed to watch G and PG shows by myself," says Eric Fowler, 9, of McLean, Virginia. "But shows that rate TV-14, I have to watch with my mom and dad." This is exactly the kind of parent involvement that the new system encourages.

Ratings War *(cont.)*

Directions: Answer the questions. You may look at the article.

1. What is the V-chip? How does it work?

2. How are the ratings supposed to help parents and kids make wise TV choices?

3. Summarize how the ratings system works. What are the codes and what do they mean?

4. How is the V-chip an example of technology being used to provide more information and support for parents raising their children?

5. What evidence can you find that the V-chip will actually work? Does the author provide evidence in the article? Explain your answer with examples.

6. Predict what you think will come after the V-chip. What is next? What else needs to be invented to address this issue?

7. What if you were the head of a television company? How would you feel about the V-chip being used to describe the content of your shows? Explain your answer.

8. Do you agree with the concept of the V-chip? Do you think it will work? How do your parents monitor what you watch?

Ratings War *(cont.)*

In 1997, the television industry began using a TV ratings system to give parents more information about what was in the shows on television. These ratings were meant to rate the shows based on their amount of violence, sex, and bad language. Here is what a TV rating means:

Audience:

This tells you for which audience the television show is meant.

Content Label:

This tells you how much violence, sex, or bad language is found in the television show.

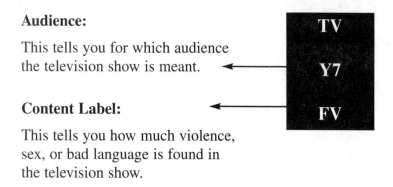

Other TV Ratings

TV Y—These programs are designed for all children. The themes and elements in the show are geared for a very young audience.

TV Y7—These programs are designed for children age 7 and above.

TV Y7 FV—These programs contain fantasy violence, but appropriate for children age 7 and up.

TV G—These programs are appropriate for all ages.

TV PG—These programs contain some materials that parents may want to watch with younger children.

TV 14—These programs contain materials that parents may find unsuitable for children age 14 years and younger. Parents are strongly cautioned.

TV MA—The program is designed for adults and is not suitable for children age 17 and younger.

---

1. When did the television industry begin the rating system? Why do you think it was started?

2. Explain the TV rating symbols above. What does the Y7 mean? What does the FV mean?

3. Is the television rating system successful? What are the strengths and weaknesses of this system?

4. What would you suggest parents do to monitor the television shows that their children watch? What would you suggest to the television industry and the government?

Ratings War *(cont.)*

Document-Based Extension Activities

Work independently or in a small group to complete the following.

1. Begin a collection of information on the V-chip and the new television ratings system. Look through newspapers, magazines, or the Internet to find articles, essays, editorial cartoons, or pictures on the topic. What is the general consensus? How can you determine the validity of this information? How can you determine what information is accurate and current?

2. Use this information to write a paper on the television ratings system. What are television ratings? How do they work? What do both sides of the issue believe about the effectiveness of television ratings?

3. How can people use the ratings system as a political advantage or to push their cause? How can the issue of television ratings be used to prevent others from doing certain activities or watching certain shows?

4. Create a survey you can use to poll students on their understanding of television ratings. Be sure to survey a large number of students to get an accurate view. Use the same survey to poll adults. What are the results? Is there a difference between adults and students on this topic? Why do you think this is so?

5. Interview people that work at television stations. Have these experts explain the debate as to whether or not television ratings are effective and if they are needed. Why are some people in business opposed to television ratings?

6. Analyze your findings. Look at the results of your polling, the interviews, and the research. Are television ratings effective? Is there evidence to prove it? Write an essay on your opinion. Be sure to reference your research. Include all of your evidence and findings as examples in your essay.

7. Post your essay on the school's Internet Web site, if you have one. Encourage other students to respond. See what the response will be.

A Communist Party!

Boom! Boom! Boom! Fifty canons thundered a salute. Jets roared across the sky, leaving behind red, blue, and gold streaks. Hundreds of tanks and rockets and 11,000 soldiers paraded, while thousands of children waved red and gold fans. On October 1, 1999, Tianenman Square in Beijing, China became a sea of color and activity. It was all part of a huge 50th anniversary party that the government threw for itself, at a cost of $36 million.

Fifty years before, on October 1, 1949, Mao Zedong (Maow Zay-dung) marched victoriously into Tianenman Square. He announced, "The People's Republic of China is founded!" Mao changed China from a country of peasant farmers and rich landowners to a country governed by communism, a system in which the government owns all the property.

In the past 50 years, China has seen many changes. In 1949, the life expectancy there was 35 years; today it is 71. Then, many Chinese went hungry; today, many are prosperous. But prosperity has come at a price.

The communist government tightly controls how people lead their lives. Freedoms are limited. Political opposition is not allowed. Those who oppose the government are put in jail.

The October celebration highlighted China's military might and gave its leaders a chance to brag. The "struggle and efforts of 50 years have brought earth-shaking changes to China," exclaimed President Jiang Zemin. "Long live the great Chinese people!"

A Communist Party! *(cont.)*

Directions: Answer the questions. You may look at the article.

1. How many years ago was the People's Republic of China started (from the time the article was written)?

2. What are some of the changes that have taken place in those years?

3. Draw a picture of what the anniversary party looked like on Tianenman Square.

4. Describe how the Chinese government was able to make the changes in China.

5. What kind of party is the article referring to? Is there a hidden or a double meaning?

6. What do you think of how the Chinese government operates? What suggestions would you make?

7. How do you predict the Chinese government will be run for the next 50 years? Will things remain the same? What differences will take place?

8. What is the most important thing for a citizen of a country? Freedom? Health? Prosperity? Protection? Explain your answer.

A Communist Party! *(cont.)*

China is not the first communist country. The Soviet Union also exercised communism for many years. Below is the flag of China. Flags are made to symbolize things about a country or state. Use the flag to answer the questions at the bottom of the page.

The flag of China is red with gold stars. The red represents the revolution. The large gold star represents the communist government of China. The smaller gold stars represent the four classes united by the common program: the workers, the peasants, the petty bourgeois, and the patriotic capitalists. This flag became the national flag of China in 1949.

1. What do the stars on this flag represent?

2. Why do you think one star is larger than the others? What does that mean?

3. Compare this flag to the United States flag. How are the flags different? How are they similar?

4. Do the flags represent the way the governments of China and United States are set up? Explain your answer.

A Communist Party! (cont.)

Document-Based Extension Activities

Work independently or in a small group to complete the following.

1. What is communism? Research communism and write the definition in your own words. Write a question/answer page that first lists questions that people might have about communism. Then after researching, record the answers that go with the questions.

2. Get a copy of a black and white world map. Color in the countries on this map that once were communist countries. Using a different color, color in the countries on the map that practice communism today. Create a key for your map. Be sure to color code countries correctly. You will need to research this information prior to completing the map.

3. Compare and contrast your country and China or another communist country. How are the two countries alike? How are they different? Create a Venn diagram to show these similarities and differences.

4. How can changing the government change the quality for its citizens? Create a list of benefits you receive as a result of being a citizen of your country. Then share your list with an older person, someone who has lived in this country longer than you have. What benefits can they add to the list? Ask them to share their feelings about living in this country.

5. Write a letter to the president or leader of your country. What suggestions would you offer to improve the life of the citizens in your country? How should your government change? What are the weaknesses and the strong points of your government? How much do you know about your government?

6. Make a list of the pros and cons of a communist government. Why might somebody want to live in a communist country? Why wouldn't somebody want to live in a communist country?

7. Research how the countries that used to be part of the Soviet Union have changed. How are these countries doing today? How are the citizens of these countries doing? Write an informational essay on these countries.

8. Locate current newspaper articles about China. What are these articles saying? What types of problems are happening in China? Are these problems a result of being a communist country?

Not Too Young to Fight

One day when Kory Johnson was 12, she called her school and said she was too sick to attend. Whoops! The next day, her picture was all over the newspaper. She had spent the day protesting a hazardous-waste-burning factory near her home in Phoenix, Arizona.

Luckily, Kory's teachers weren't too angry. Her protest helped stop pollution in the school's own backyard. Since then she has challenged other big companies to stop polluting. Now 20, Kory gives hope to kids everywhere that they can successfully fight for the good of the planet.

Kory was nine when her sister died from heart factors that her family believes were caused by chemicals in the drinking water. Kory discovered that other people in the area had health problems that might be related to pollution. She grew angry that her neighborhood was used as a dumping ground for toxic waste.

Kory decided to take action. The fourth-grader created a group called Children for a Safe Environment (CSE). Kory was working with CSE when she learned about the toxic-waste plant that was about to open in Phoenix. With a lot of hard work, CSE persuaded the Arizona government to buy the $44 million factory and stop it from running. "We fought for two full years," remembers Kory. When CSE finally won, "it seemed too good to be true!"

In 1990, she turned her attention to McDonald's to stop packing its fast food in Styrofoam, which stays on the earth for good once it is manufactured. CSE unloaded three refrigerator boxes full of Styrofoam on the front lawn of Joan Kroc, whose husband founded the McDonald's chain! The fast-food giant soon switched to the more environment-friendly packing it uses today.

Kory has also educated her community about recycling and how to fight back against industries that pollute poor neighborhoods. Since 1988, about 300 kids have joined CSE. Most of them live in poor neighborhoods that are targets for bad environmental practices. They have inspired other children in the U.S. to form similar organizations, and they often ask Kory for tips on how to bring about change.

What advice does she have for kids who want to become heroes for the planet? "Find out anything you can do to help," she says. "One kid can make a difference, even if it's the smallest thing you start."

Kory has won many awards for her heroic work. In 1998 she won a Goldman Prize, one of the world's most important environmental honors. As one of six winners, Kory received $100,000. Getting that much money is "scary," she says. She is still trying to decide how to spend it wisely.

Thanks to Kory's hard work, the future looks brighter for folks in her neighborhood. Now at college, she's not sure what her future holds: "I take it one day at a time." One thing is certain: she won't stop fighting for a cleaner, healthier planet. Kory says, "I'm in it for life."

Not Too Young to Fight (cont.)

Directions: Answer the questions. You may look at the article.

1. What was the real reason that Kory Johnson missed school that day?

2. What motivated Kory to get involved in her organization?

3. How does the author feel about the work that Kory is doing? Summarize what the author thinks, using examples from the text.

4. Describe what it would feel like to be involved in making changes to protect the environment and our health. How does Kory feel about this?

5. Draw a time line using small pictures showing the progression Kory Johnson has taken to get her to where she is now. Is there an organization like hers in your city?

6. Obviously, Kory Johnson has found success in her efforts. List the reasons why you think that Kory is effective.

7. Prepare a plan for a project that can be done to improve the quality of air, water, or land in your town or city. Use the tips and ideas from Kory Johnson and her experience.

8. What if Kory had never gotten involved? How would things be different in Phoenix, Arizona?

9. What could you say to convince your community to get involved? Write a letter to convince your local officials on the importance of the environment.

Not Too Young to Fight (cont.)

Kory has started an organization to help other kids get involved in saving the environment. Other organizations throughout the country have also been set up. Below is a fictional letter written by a child who shares strong feelings about taking care of the pollution in our country. In 1990, a letter similar to this one was posted on 250 billboards throughout the United States. The letter was written by a nine-year-old girl named Melissa Poe. She was determined to save the environment. Use the letter to answer the questions at the bottom of the page.

Dear Mr. President,

We are worried about our earth! We need to keep it clean if we want to keep living on it. I want to live for a very long time.

Are you willing to do something about it? If you don't, then we will die of all the pollution. Please help us!

Sincerely,

Franklin Deitz

---

1. What is the purpose of putting a letter like this on billboards?

2. How does Franklin Deitz feel about the environment? How can you tell?

3. Why does Franklin state "that we will die" if we don't keep the earth clean?

4. Explain why a billboard like this might make a difference.

5. Do you think these billboards have made a difference for the environment? Why or why not?

Not Too Young to Fight *(cont.)*

Document-Based Extension Activities

Work independently or in a small group to complete the following.

1. Design a brochure on keeping the environment safe. Utilize the information from the Environmental Protection Agency in your brochure.

2. Draw a cause-and-effect graphic to show what happens when people don't take care of the environment.

3. Locate Phoenix on a map of Arizona. How do things going on in Arizona affect you in your city or state? Do the environmental concerns have an impact on other states in the area or ones far away?

4. Write a letter to Kory Johnson asking questions of her work and efforts. Ask her what you can do to further the cause of keeping the environment clean and healthy. Design letterhead you can use to print your letter.

5. Make a list of things you can do to preserve the environment. Make a poster to portray this list. Remember to use a large font size and bold-face type to highlight certain information and to emphasize important points.

6. Write a cause-and-effect essay using the information you have gathered and learned about the environment. Some questions to consider as you write your essay might include:

   - What is wrong with polluting the environment?
   - What is the cause of these problems?
   - What are the effects of polluting the environment?
   - What are some suggestions to fixing the dirty environment?
   - What are the factors that need to be taken into consideration when putting a plan of prevention together?

Do Kids Look Up to Athletes Too Much?

Yes

Kids see athletes on TV all of the time. They not only play in games but also appear in commercials and talk shows. Some kids think that athletes are heroes, even though the kids have never met the athletes. They need to learn that just because a person is a success in a professional sport does not mean that person will be a good role model in other ways.

Athletes and companies that sell athletic clothing, soft drinks, and other products make money when kids look up to athletes. Kids want to wear the shoes and drink the drinks that are advertised by the athlete. It's too bad that lots of kids waste their money this way. What's even worse is when kids copy other behaviors of the athlete. Kids could end up getting tattoos, dying their hair, or even taking drugs because an athlete does those things.

Athletes are simply regular people who play sports. Kids need to learn that having a special athletic talent does not always make a person special in other ways. Kids should stop getting carried away with worshipping athletes. They should see that their parents, teachers, and other caring adults are the best role models.

No

Professional athletes have more than just great talent. They have worked very hard to be at the top of their sport. Who could be better role models than people like Michael Jordan or Wayne Gretzky, who have worked hard and reached a goal?

Some kids like to wear the jerseys of their favorite athletes. This doesn't mean the kids are getting carried away by hero worship. Most kids have several role models, including parents and teachers. There's room for athletes as role models, too. Besides, some kids don't have people at home to admire. They need good role models.

Kids are smart enough to admire athletes who are good people off the field as well as on it. They admire athletes who try their hardest, show good sportsmanship, and are nice to people on and off the field. They reject athletes who argue or fight during games. They also reject athletes who take drugs or get in other trouble off the field.

Most kids don't feel they must wear the same clothes, hats, and shoes as their favorite athletes. Instead, they respect one or two athletes because of their behavior on and off the field. That's not going overboard!

Do Kids Look Up to Athletes Too Much? *(cont.)*

Directions: Answer the questions. You may look at the article.

1. State the two viewpoints mentioned in this article.

2. Describe in your own words why one author feels that athletes are not good role models.

3. Why is it significant that athletes are being evaluated as to whether or not they make good role models?

4. What evidence can you list for athletes being good role models?

5. Identify the motive for the author stating that athletes are not always good role models.

6. What ideas can you add to either viewpoint presented in this article?

7. Which viewpoint do you agree with? Explain your answer.

8. Which viewpoint do you think was most persuasive and effective? Explain your answer.

Do Kids Look Up to Athletes Too Much? *(cont.)*

What do kids think about the subject of role models? Read the fictional editorial written by a kid. Use the editorial to answer the questions at the bottom of the page.

Who Are Our Role Models?

by Ashley, age 14, Junior Editor

Just what is a role model? A role model is a person you look up to. A role model is someone you want to be like. A role model can be just about anyone who you deem worthy of this job. A role model to one person might be completely different for another person.

Unfortunately, not all kids are picking positive role models. Some children are choosing cartoon characters or actors from a TV show or movie. These people or characters are not always doing good things. Some kids are even picking role models that are real life people, such as an older student or teacher. This is good as long as the actions of the role model are positive and uplifting.

Kids are even picking role models that they are not aware of. They might look up to someone without realizing it. For many kids, their parents can serve as role models. Again, this is good as long as the parents are positive, uplifting individuals.

Who you pick as a role model can say a lot about who you are as a person. People doing the things that you are interested in are often the people you select to admire. The best role model is someone that helps you want to be a better person.

Role models are the most important thing in a child's life when growing up. Everyone needs someone to admire. Have you ever thought that you might be a role model? You could be a role model some day. You might even be one now to a younger brother, sister, relative, or friend. Set positive examples for kids to follow. Try to be the best role model you can be.

1. What is the message in this editorial? How does the author feel about role models?

2. How does the author feel about negative role models? What does the author suggest as criteria to use to determine whether a person is a positive role model or not?

3. What qualities do you think someone should have in order to be a good role model?

4. Who do you think the author of this editorial has as a role model? Explain your answer.

Do Kids Look Up to Athletes Too Much? *(cont.)*

Document-Based Extension Activities

Work independently or in a small group to complete the following.

1. Imagine that your group has been given the assignment to determine whether or not kids should look up to athletes. What is needed to determine the pros and cons of using athletes as role models? As a group, brainstorm what information you would need to determine the role model qualities of an athlete.

2. Look back at the article. What did the authors consider before writing their essay? Make a list of these items and use them in your own research.

3. Research how the kids can be affected by using athletes as role models. Are there any famous athletes in your community? How do children respond to the famous athletes? Interview personnel via e-mail or in person to gather their input on the topic of children looking up to athletes.

4. Create a survey that you can use to poll students in your school about this topic. Be sure to survey a large number of students to get an accurate view. Use the same survey to poll the teachers and administrators at your school, as well as a large sample of parents. What are the results?

5. Interview the school administrators to find out how role models affect the behavior of students. Does the administrator see a difference in the behavior of the student based on who the role model is?

6. See if you can set up an interview with a parent. Talk with the parent about why selecting the right role model is so important. Encourage the parent to share the experiences that he or she had while growing up based on who he/she chose as a role model.

7. Write a cause-and-effect essay using the information you have gathered and learned about role models. Some questions to consider as you write your essay might include:

   • Who are your role models? What kind of people are they?

   • Do your role models change with age?

   • Do you look to your parents as role models? Why or why not?

   • How can you get a child to change who his/her role model is?

Answer Key

Many of the answers to the questions in this series are subjective. There may be a different answer that your student used to answer the questions. Please note that these answers are suggestions and can be modified as needed.

Page 17
1. They made them mandatory to try to reduce violence and improve students' grades.
2. The uniform is navy pants, shorts or skirt with a white shirt.
3. Students should state whether or not the students in their school would approve of the uniforms and give a reason explaining why.
4. Illustrations will vary. Students should explain why students would love to wear it.
5. Students should list at least two or three things that are similar and different between their school and the one mentioned in the article. Differences and similarities might include size, what students wear to school, the amount of violence in their school, student attitudes towards uniforms, parent support of uniforms, etc.
6. Answers will vary. Responses should include both a pro and a con.
7. Answers will vary. Responses should include the author's opinion along with evidence or reasons explaining the answer.
8. Answers will vary. Responses should include examples from the "Fearless Fashion" article to support an opinion.
9. Answers will vary. Responses should specifically address whether or not the student feels the clothes worn by students can affect the amount of crime, fighting, and suspensions in schools.

Page 18
1. It appears that violence has declined in the school district. School uniforms are a variable that has changed. It can be assumed that school uniforms curb violence and other negative influences at school.
2. They did their research. They looked into other districts and countries using school uniforms.
3. Answers will vary. Students should have at least five to ten questions on their survey.

Page 21
1. The earthquake happened in Turkey on August 17, 1999.
2. It was scary. Some people felt like they were going to pass out.
3. A fault line is a huge underground crack.
4. Answers will vary.
5. Answers will vary.
6. Answers will vary.
7. Some people build on a fault line because that is where they were raised. They have no other place to live. They may not know they live on a fault line. Some people don't believe that an earthquake will really happen.
8. Answers will vary. People might have been hurt more because they would have been up and out in the streets.
9. Answers will vary.
10. Answers will vary. Look for well thought out answers.

Page 22
1. the Black Sea and the Mediterranean Sea
2. Answers will vary. They are both next to bodies of water. They are both built on fault lines.
3. Answers will vary. They should keep people informed. They should ensure that buildings meet the codes to withstand an earthquake. They should have a plan to care for people in times of an earthquake.
4. Answers will vary. The government should be prepared and ready to help in any way necessary. They should be willing to spend money.

Page 25
1. She's trying to protect them from being shot by poachers.
2. Yes; now about 200 birds are shot.
3. They go on hunting patrol. More and more birds will be saved.
4. They yelled insults, mailed her a dead falcon, and set her car on fire.
5. Because of the abuse from the poachers, law enforcers began to see Giordano's cause.
6. Answers will vary.
7. The poachers can be arrested and tracked down.
8. She goes on hunting patrol. She is raising funds for a bird center in Italy. She works at the WWF Center for the Rehabilitation of Injured Birds.
9. Answers will vary. Answers may include dedicated, compassionate, committed, hard working, fearless.

Page 26
1. It is to improve the environment in which animals live and to keep their habitats protected.
2. Answers will vary. Ask a teacher. Look it up in a book. Research it on the Internet. Use context clues from this letter.
3. Answers will vary. The letter will probably show support for their efforts.
4. She would be interested in any projects that save and protect the habitats of birds and other animals. Answers will vary. Student lists should include organizations they are aware of that have similar goals.

Page 29
1. Because they are wild, sharp-toothed creatures.
2. 1995; to help balance Yellowstone's ecosystem
3. Take it to another judge. Appeal the case.
4. They are afraid they will kill all of their livestock and make it impossible to raise cattle.
5. Answers will vary. Pros – Balance ecosystem, wolves are no longer extinct in Yellowstone. Cons – They pose threats to humans and livestock.
6. Grizzly bears no longer strip the trees as they can eat the wolves' leftovers. There are fewer coyotes because the wolves have killed some. More rodents are available for foxes, badgers, and eagles to eat. Trees and plants are healthier.
7. Answers will vary.
8. Answers will vary. Responses might include the fact that he thinks the wolves should remain in Yellowstone.
9. Answers will vary. Answer should contain justifiable explanation and support.

Page 30
1. "Little Red Riding Hood" and "The Three Little Pigs"
2. The message is that it is a good thing the wolves have returned and it is about time.
3. Answers will vary. Responses should include support for their answers.
4. Answers will vary. Mother Goose would be telling a story about how the wolves found a better place to live than Yellowstone. And of course they lived happily ever after.

Answer Key (cont.)

Page 33
1. to clean up the vacant lot; Twenty people were involved.
2. He divided up the lot into 4 parts and assigned 5 people to work on each quadrant.
3. At first he was hesitant, but by the end he thought it was a good idea. The list might include: ". . . rather been anywhere else, awful mess, hot, sweaty, grimy." "I like to go there! Proud, good thing, pretty patch of green, enjoy . . ."
4. hard, sweaty, tiring, fulfilling, rewarding
5. One end of the time line should show that the lot had slimy, fast-food wraps, old newspaper, and trash. The other end should show flowers and vegetables.
6. You can visibly see the progress and improvements. People were working together toward a common goal.
7. You wouldn't want to read it. It's boring to hear someone griping.
8. Answers will vary. Look for a well thought out, organized plan.
9. Answers will vary.

Page 34
1. This sign is advertising a potluck party for the neighbors that worked on the vacant lot together. Yes. It will be successful. It is a celebration of their hard work.
2. They are proud and pleased with their efforts. Their work has brought them closer together.
3. They have cleaned the vacant lot. They are planning to have a potluck party together. They plan on coming to the potluck party with ideas for more neighborhood projects.
4. Answers will vary. They involved the young and the old. They worked together towards making life in the neighborhood better.

Page 37
1. He feels they should become a state.
2. 900 miles southeast of Miami; It was discovered by Christopher Columbus in 1493.
3. 46% voted in favor. Not quite the majority. There are a lot of hesitant voters.
4. As in the other states, English is the dominant language and Spanish might lose its popularity and strength.
5. U.S. – Relationship would be easier. U.S. citizens would enjoy learning about and experiencing the culture of Puerto Rico. Puerto Rico – Receive full citizenship benefits. Become part of the booming U.S. economy.
6. Answers will vary.
7. Answers will vary. Look for explanations to support student answer.
8. Answers will vary. Look for a well thought out, organized plan.
9. Answers will vary.

Page 38
1. They would get on a ship or take a plane and fly 900 miles southeast. They would pass Cuba, Haiti, and the Dominican Republic.
2. It would be close to other small nations of interest. It would be a good vacation spot for visitors.
3. It is pretty far from the mainland, which would make it difficult. Gaining access would take time and money.
4. Answers will vary. Students need to support their opinion.
5. Answers will vary. Encourage students to write a well-written and thought out plan.

Page 41
1. teachers; They perform an important job.
2. Teaches tirelessly and expertly all day. She spends personal money. She volunteers her personal time on the weekend.
3. to be rewarded for their efforts and commitment
4. There will need to be a good way to recruit good teachers to fill these positions.
5. Yes. It indicates that enough time has gone by. It's urgent!
6. Answers will vary.
7. Answers will vary. Suggestions might include to accept donations from companies or write grants.
8. Answers will vary.

Page 42
1. $35,227; $38,950
2. Answers will vary. Salaries will probably increase as they show on the chart.
3. Yes. Wisconsin can say that their teacher salaries continue to improve.
4. Answers will vary. Look for creative solutions to teacher salaries.

Page 45
1. It is designed by kids and has different creatures than the usual carousel.
2. Milo Mottola and children created it. Milo Mottola provided drawing classes and selected the children. It is in Riverbank State Park in New York City.
3. Answers will vary.
4. They thought it was fun. They enjoyed Milo Mottola. They thought he was funny.
5. He held drawing classes in the park. Children drew pictures. He had to choose from 1,000 drawings. Originals are hung above each animal.
6. It has thirty-two animals and two chariots.
7. Answers will vary. Look for reasonable description incorporating both futuristic and medieval theme.
8. Answers will vary. Look for a well thought out and organized plan.
9. Answers will vary.

Page 46
1. At first, he thought it wouldn't be quality work. This is a common impression of things done by kids because kids are just learning.
2. He thinks it's great. Some words he uses are *professionally done, kudos, Wow!,* and *amazed.*
3. Get more projects going in the community that involve kids. Answers will vary.
4. Answers will vary. Look for letters that include examples to back up their ideas.

Page 49
1. a caver; Geologists study rocks and speleologists study caves.
2. It is full of animals that have adapted to living underground.
3. She loves it! She likes the exploration and the adventure.
4. Answers will vary. It has living animals.
5. They can look at her example of going for her goals and dreams.
6. Most animals can't live under such conditions.
7. She would have missed out on her life calling—adventure! Answers will vary.
8. Answers will vary. Both!
9. Answers will vary. Is she doing what she has always wanted to do? Is she happy?

Answer Key (cont.)

Page 50
1. The picture is inside a cave.
2. Answers may vary. Some answers might include getting lost, getting hurt, falling, getting bit by animals at the entrance, etc.
3. Answers will vary. Perhaps head lamps, chisel, hammer, and ropes.
4. Answers will vary.

Page 53
1. Noel is a male runner about the age of the author.
2. It has trees, winding painted path, a forest, etc.
3. Noel accidentally dragged his spiked shoe down the back of Cliff's leg. Noel zipped on ahead to victory.
4. He doesn't like him. He doesn't want to be around him.
5. It showed he was sincere in his apology.
6. There was no reason for Noel to do this. Eventually he is convinced.
7. Answers will vary.
8. Answers will vary. Let it go – You can't hold onto these feelings.
9. Answers will vary. He is compassionate and sincere.

Page 54
1. The main idea of the letter is to apologize.
2. Answers will vary.
3. Answers will vary.
4. Answers will vary. Responses should have support to back up their predictions.

Page 57
1. 4,000 square miles
2. Freshwater marsh, river and swamp; The Everglades is a unique ecosystem in Florida.
3. Because it is disappearing. She shows how sacred the Everglades are.
4. 56 animal species are threatened or endangered. Some animals have vanished.
5. Sugar growers use fertilizers which cause damage. There is also the damage of draining the water in the past.
6. Answers will vary. Order no more use of phosphorous.
7. Businesses would adapt. They might lose money. The ecosystem would flourish.
8. Answers will vary. Look for evidence that supports the student's answer.
9. Answers will vary. The author explains the history and then gives the current conditions. Look for student response to offer suggestions.

Page 58
1. poisonous and nonpoisonous snakes
2. There are more non-poisonous snakes found in the Everglades. The number of snakes will decrease.
3. Answers will vary. Each animal, dangerous or not, plays an important role in the ecosystem.
4. Answers will vary. Look for responses that include an explanation for their answer.

Page 61
1. The lions were sick. One thousand died.
2. Canine distemper
3. They got it from the hyenas which may have picked up the germs at village dumps visited by dogs.
4. They are raising money to vaccinate dogs living in the park.
5. The lions won't get sick and die off.
6. Answers will vary. Look for step-by-step answers.
7. Answers will vary.
8. Answers will vary.

Page 62
1. The purpose of this brochure is to inform the public about mountain lions. You can learn a description, the habitat, and the number of mountain lions in North America.
2. Answers will vary. Responses should include the different places where lions are found, different eating habits, exposure to the canine distemper, etc.
3. Answers will vary.
4. Answers will vary. Responses should include examples of how cities and towns affect wildlife.

Page 65
1. He was an explorer. He was planning to be the first person to travel across Antarctica.
2. He and his crew got stranded and got caught in severe icebergs for nearly ten months. He ended up being a hero and saving his crew.
3. Answers will vary.
4. He realized they were in danger.
5. Answers will vary.
6. Answers will vary.
7. Answers will vary. They were probably overjoyed, and filled with relief and gratitude.
8. Answers will vary. Answers may include overcoming hardship, inspiration.

Page 66
1. about ten months
2. The map shows the dates and places where Shackleton and his crew began, got stuck, and sailed for help. Weddell Sea and the Atlantic Ocean
3. Answers will vary.

Page 69
1. birds
2. He found fossilized bones. The fossils might belong to a dinosaur with feathers.
3. Answers will vary. Feathers might offer warmth and protection.
4. Some scientists think they may be bits and pieces of scales.
5. Two different viewpoints can keep options open. We can continue to look at new ideas.
6. the finding of more fossilized dinosaur bones with feathers
7. Answers will vary. Students should show examples from the text to support their opinion.
8. Answers will vary. Students should determine realistic criteria.

Page 70
1. the chicken and the sinosauropteryx prima; There seem to be more differences.
2. They can learn about how dinosaurs might have lived and what may have caused their extinction.
3. Answers will vary.
4. Scientists need lots of evidence to prove that dinosaurs had feathers. Scientists gain evidence by doing years and years of research.

Page 73
1. Greenland
2. homes set up by Vikings
3. He wanted help getting the sea life. He chose the name to get them to think it was a green, lush island.
4. Answers will vary.
5. Artifacts such as kitchen utensils, necklaces, dice, miniature boats and wooden boxes.
6. Answers will vary. The weather got worse and trade dried up. Europe was no longer interested in what Greenland had to offer.

Answer Key *(cont.)*

Page 73 *(cont.)*

7. Answers will vary. Answers may include the idea that Greenland would be more established.
8. Answers may vary. Scientists have been trained to know what to look for and they know what a civilization would need for survival.
9. Answers will vary. Look for evidence to support the opinion.

Page 74

1. The shield and helmet are for protection. The Vikings needed armor for their travels and their adventures. They lived a rough life and lived in extreme conditions and temperatures.
2. A Viking would need to have endurance, commitment, bravery, skill, and perseverance.
3. It must have been very cold and harsh; lots of wind, snow, rain, and water.
4. Answers will vary. Responses should list similarities and differences.

Page 77

1. He works on animal teeth.
2. He has treated over 50 species in all.
3. He was asked by a veterinarian to pull some teeth from a cat. At first he thought he would never do that again. He possibly felt needed. Answers may vary.
4. He realizes the importance of having healthy teeth.
5. Answers may vary. Animals can't tell you when it hurts. It might be dangerous.
6. Answers will vary. Look for reasonable similarities and differences between humans and animal teeth.
7. Answers will vary. Some animals clean their teeth by what they eat.
8. Answers will vary. Comparisons help us relate to new information.
9. Answers will vary. Because he is a dentist, you consider his advice professional, and it makes it all seem more personal.

Page 78

1. Lion teeth are much longer and sharper.
2. Answers will vary. Responses should include both pros and cons.
3. Answers will vary.
4. Answers will vary. Answers should include examples of what lions eat as evidence.

Page 81

1. They are duck-billed platypuses. They live in a sanctuary in Melbourne, Australia.
2. It took six months.
3. The last time a platypus delivered a baby in captivity was during World War II.
4. Answers will vary. Responses should include sentences and examples from the text.
5. The platypus needed privacy, plenty of food, and protection.
6. Answers will vary. The platypus needs the conditions to be just right in order to reproduce.
7. Yes. History would have been made, but it would not be very significant because the babies had not lived. There would probably not have been an article in a magazine spotlighting them.
8. Fisk is knowledgeable, experienced, and extremely patient.
9. Answers will vary. Responses should include specific advice and examples showing understanding of ideas presented in the text.

Page 82

1. A platypus lives in a damp, moist, grassy area near a pool of water.
2. A platypus would probably eat bugs and other things that live near water and grass.
3. A platypus needs its environment to be just right. The right amount of moisture, food, temperature, and climate.
4. Answers will vary. Answers might include getting the materials, the work to build it, the support needed, and getting help from experts.

Page 85

1. Choctaw is a language of the Native American Choctaw tribe.
2. An endangered language is a language at risk of being lost or forgotten. People stop speaking the language.
3. He realizes the importance of this language staying "alive." He knows the language and feels an obligation to keep it going.
4. Money is needed to preserve a language by recording or documenting the language.
5. She seems to enjoy learning it.
6. Answers will vary. Ensure that responses have support to back up their opinion.
7. Governments may not want people to speak their native language because they can't understand it and it makes it hard to communicate.
8. Answers will vary. Post them on the Internet.
9. Most people don't know about these endangered languages. This knowledge can help make people more aware. The purpose of this article is to inform others.

Page 86

1. the Choctaw language of the Native American tribe and the English language
2. "Halito. Chim achukma? Salaha hosh anumpoli."
3. Answers will vary.
4. Answers will vary. The Choctaw language looks like a complicated language. If there are few people that speak it, and it is difficult to learn, then the chance of preservation will be slim.

Page 89

1. because it contains too much sugar that harms our bodies and provides no nutrients
2. They spent $750 million.
3. Milk contains vitamins and minerals. Soda doesn't contain anything healthy, and so kids are not getting nutrients they need.
4. Florida; The money from soda sales helps support school budgets.
5. Answers will vary.
6. Answers will vary.
7. Answers will vary. Selling soda wouldn't be as important.
8. Answers will vary. Look for a well-balanced letter.
9. Answers will vary.

Page 90

1. about 15 ounces of milk
2. Boys drink more soda. Reasons will vary.
3. Answers will vary. Responses should include support for their answer.
4. Answers will vary. Kids will not be getting important vitamins and minerals that milk provides. Illnesses may increase, there may be more obese kids, etc.

Answer Key *(cont.)*

Page 93

1. The V-chip allows parents to screen out any shows they don't want their kids to watch.
2. The ratings system is to give parents information they need to monitor the shows their kids watch.
3. Shows are rated based on the content it contains. G (everyone), PG (parental guidance suggested), TV-14 (kids 14 and older), TV-M (mature audiences)
4. With the V-chip, parents have a way of keeping their children from watching certain shows.
5. Parents say that it has helped. The article cites examples from parents.
6. Answers will vary.
7. Answers will vary. Be sure students explain their answer.
8. Answers will vary. Responses should include description of how their television watching is monitored at home.

Page 94

1. It began in 1997. People were concerned over what their children were watching on television. They were looking for a way to inform parents.
2. The symbol *Y7* shows that the television show is meant for children age 7 and above. The *FV* means there is fantasy violence.
3. Answers will vary.
4. Answers will vary. Parents could watch television shows with their children. The television industry could air shows that aren't appropriate for children only late at night.

Page 97

1. fifty years (started in 1949)
2. The People's Republic of China was founded and became governed by communism.
3. Pictures will vary.
4. The government tightened control of how people lived their lives.
5. The author is referring to a party thrown by a political party. There is a hidden meaning indicating that the anniversary was a party and that the Chinese government is worth celebrating.
6. Answers will vary. Be sure students include suggestions in their answers.
7. Answers will vary. Responses should include explanation for their response.
8. Answers will vary. Responses should be well thought out and thorough.

Page 98

1. the government and the classes of people in China
2. The government is all-powerful, in charge, and in authority.
3. The U.S. flag has fifty stars set equally on the flag. Both flags have stars and contain red.
4. Yes. Answers will vary. Responses should explain how U.S. government has shared power. China has set roles for people with less freedom to choose.

Page 101

1. She was protesting.
2. Her sister died of heart problems that she thinks were related to their drinking water.
3. The author thinks that more kids should get involved. Answers will vary.
4. Answers will vary. Kory loves being involved. She believes she can make a difference.
5. Answers will vary.
6. Answers will vary. Kory is determined, willing to fight, and spends time and energy when needed.
7. Answers will vary. Responses should be a well thought out plan.
8. There might be a hazardous-waste-burning factory, as well as other similar facilities, near her home.
9. Answers will vary.

Page 102

1. Get the people's attention on the issue.
2. He is concerned. He says we'll die. He's worried!
3. Severe pollution can cause death and he is trying to show how serious the issue is.
4. It might encourage people to write letters, get involved, or get angry.
5. Answers will vary. If no, people are aware of the environment already. If yes, more and more people need to help save our environment.

Page 105

1. One person thinks kids look up to athletes too much. The other person thinks it is completely okay to look up to athletes.
2. Because athletes do not always set good examples or make good decisions.
3. Because role models can make a big difference in a kid's life and athletes are set up as role models for kids.
4. Many athletes set examples of excellence, skill, determination, hard work, etc.
5. Not all athletes are good examples. They may be doing drugs, getting tattoos, or using foul language.
6. Answers will vary.
7. Answers will vary.
8. Answers will vary. Answers should include evidence.

Page 106

1. Role models are important. It's important to pick the right ones.
2. They are doing harm to kids. Someone who gets you to be positive and uplifting.
3. Answers will vary. Answers might include honesty, hard working, and morals.
4. Her parents, a teacher—answers will vary. Have students explain their answer.